Praise for *What Grea*

In my 30+ years of working with pastors around the world, I've never seen this level of personal anxiety and insecurity as we face the challenges and pressures of this kairos moment. We need strong local churches more than ever. *What Great Ministry Leaders Get Right* lays out the foundational qualities pastors and ministry leaders need in these challenging times. Based on years of dedicated research with hundreds of pastors, it's full of practical examples and guidance that can fill in the gaps of what gets missed in seminary. Every one of us has weak spots in our pastoral leadership. This book can help us become more joyful, confident, and fruitful as we fulfill our part in building Christ's kingdom.

KEVIN PALAU
President and CEO of Luis Palau Association

There are a thousand demands on a ministry leader's time and attention. But what are the things that great ministry leaders do that make them truly effective? I'm grateful for my friends Jimmy and Renaut for writing this book *What Great Ministry Leaders Get Right*. It's an important guide for any ministry leader who wants to do great work, not for their own glory but for the glory of God and His coming kingdom.

ED STETZER
Executive Director of the Billy Graham Center at Wheaton College

Anyone in leadership learns quickly that people are usually eager to identify what you're doing wrong. Compliments are harder to come by; solid, time-tested advice for what works best is rarer still. Whether you've been leading for years or are just starting out, you'll find treasures of wisdom in these pages that will strengthen your ministry and help you serve *better*.

JIM DALY
President, Focus on the Family

What struck me most powerfully in reading *What Great Ministry Leaders Get Right* was its honesty. Honesty often becomes the victim of therapeutic sentimentalism. This was different. It takes standards and accountability seriously. I thought the chapter on rest, pace of life, and burnout was worth getting the book. This book will improve a lot of pastors' lives, and their families will benefit greatly.

BILL HULL
Cofounder, The Bonhoeffer Project
Author of *Conversion & Discipleship: You Can't Have One without the Other*

When ministry leaders fall, the consequences for churches and Christians are painful and destructive. When ministry leaders lead well, churches so often thrive. Paul tells Timothy in 1 Timothy 4:16 to "watch [his] life and doctrine closely" (NIV). Renaut and Jimmy's new and excellent book is a clear roadmap for applying Paul's wise advice. I am thrilled to commend this book to every ministry leader. I encourage you not only to read it carefully but also to live out the excellent advice of these two veteran ministry leaders!

BRIAN HOWARD
Executive Director, Acts 29

In *What Great Ministry Leaders Get Right*, Jimmy and Renaut intertwine practical advice and easy-to-follow core steps to create a must-read for anyone needing guidance on their own personal calling in life. This book will leave a lasting impression on the reader and equip you with the necessary tools to build a legacy worth leaving.

JOE WHITE
President of Kanakuk Kamps

As one who is passionate about the experience of resiliency among pastors, I find this book incredibly helpful. It provides handles and structural considerations for a pastor to care well for himself throughout the ups and downs of ministry. It really assists a pastor in developing his own personal plan for self-care.

DWAYNE R. BOND
Lead Pastor, Wellspring Church, Charlotte, NC
Director of Pastoral Care for the Acts 29 Network

Many ministry leaders today are struggling with feelings of inadequacy as they try to live out their callings. Jimmy Dodd and Renaut van der Riet's book *What Great Ministry Leaders Get Right* presents well-rounded and practical competencies that will help pastors lead from a place of spiritual, physical, and emotional health. This book will benefit leaders and serve as an essential supplement to seminary education.

DOUG LOGAN
President of Grimké Seminary
Associate Director of the Acts 29 Global Network
Author of *On the Block: Developing a Biblical Picture for Missional Engagement*

Think of this book as the supplementary leadership training that you wish was covered at seminary or Bible college. Written by pastors and for pastors, *What Great Ministry Leaders Get Right* by Jimmy Dodd and Renaut van der Riet is a well-written example of how Christ-centered ministry practices shape every part of our lives. With practical insights grounded in biblical wisdom, this book is a must-have on the shelf of any ministry leader.

ADAM RAMSEY
Lead Pastor at Liberti Church, Gold Coast, Australia
Network Director for Acts 29 Australia & New Zealand

After nearly a half century in ministry, I can honestly say that I wish I had read this book from the beginning. With profound practical insight and biblical truth, Jimmy and Renaut have identified the primary obstacles to flourishing as a pastor as well as the disciplines that will keep our hearts pure and devoted to church and family. But even now, as I approach that half-century mark, I can say that this book was a true blessing and encouragement. I need these guys to help me stay the course now no less than I needed them when I first launched out into ministry. So, whether you are just beginning in church leadership or, like me, you are in the homestretch, get this book and immerse yourself in its truths. I promise that you will not have wasted a second in doing so.

SAM STORMS
Bridgeway Church, Oklahoma City, OK

Even a glance at the table of contents will tell any reader that *What Great Leaders Get Right* is rich with insights from experienced pastors. It will be a great gift for those who are working on recalibrating ministry during this most disruptive moment. Offering real examples from real leaders from the front lines of ministry, there is winsome encouragement and the wisdom of experience shining through every page. Many will find, in the words of an old hymn, "strength for today and bright hope for tomorrow" in this generous compilation of insights from some of the most effective pastors.

TOD BOLSINGER
Author of *Tempered Resilience: How Leaders Are Formed in the Crucible of Change*

Though their load has never been greater, all too many pastors maintain their cars with more intentionality than their own lives and ministries. For pastors overdue for their ten-thousand-mile tune-up and needing a resource, this is your book. These twenty-four succinct—biblical, highly practical, and downright gripping—chapters will together give you the comprehensive self-evaluative tool you need.

NICHOLAS PERRIN
President of Trinity International University

Jimmy Dodd has devoted his life to ministering to ministers and to serving leaders. This book is another contribution by Dodd toward these noble ends.

JASON K. ALLEN
President of Midwestern Baptist Theological Seminary and Spurgeon College

Jimmy and Renaut bring decades of practical and frontline experience to this great resource. They are like veteran sherpas helping us know how to navigate the complexities of modern-day ministry. Any pastor who will live out these competencies will have a healthy, enduring, and effective ministry. This book will help you stay in love with Jesus and ministry.

LANCE WITT
Founder of Replenish Ministries

In a time when a growing number of ministry leaders are getting it wrong and sowing great harm in the church, *What Great Ministry Leaders Get Right* is a welcome, timely, well-researched, comprehensive, and much-needed resource. Jimmy Dodd and Renaut van der Riet destroy the ministry idol of leaders appearing to have it all together and restore a biblical understanding of whole-life discipleship and servant leadership deeply rooted in the gospel and example of Jesus. As president of a seminary seeking to equip students with this ethos and practice, I heartily recommend it as an outstanding tool for students before, during, and after their time in seminary.

MARK L. DALBEY
President and Associate Professor of Applied Theology at Covenant Seminary

Jimmy Dodd and Renaut van der Riet have provided a terrifically practical and yet comprehensive resource for ministry leaders. This is the stuff of real life, not the stuff of seminary. Read through this resource prayerfully. Where do you sense God affirming your current way of life? Where might you sense God highlighting areas that might be most important for you to address? Let the rubber meet the road on these six core competencies. Your life and ministry may well depend on it.

MINDY CALIGUIRE
Cofounder of Soul Care
Author of *Discovering Soul Care*

WHAT GREAT MINISTRY LEADERS GET RIGHT

Six Core Competencies You Need
to Succeed in Your Calling

JIMMY DODD AND RENAUT VAN DER RIET

MOODY PUBLISHERS
CHICAGO

Unless otherwise indicated, all Scripture quotations are from the ESV® Bible (The Holy Bible, English Standard Version®), copyright © 2001 by Crossway, a publishing ministry of Good News Publishers. Used by permission. All rights reserved.

Scripture quotations marked NIV are taken from the Holy Bible, New International Version®, NIV®. Copyright © 1973, 1978, 1984, 2011 by Biblica, Inc.™ Used by permission of Zondervan. All rights reserved worldwide. www.zondervan.com The "NIV" and "New International Version" are trademarks registered in the United States Patent and Trademark Office by Biblica, Inc.™

Scripture quotations marked VOICE are taken from The Voice. Copyright © 2008, 2011 by Thomas Nelson. Used by permission. All rights reserved.

Scripture quotations marked TLB are taken from The Living Bible. Copyright © 1971 by Tyndale House Publishers. Used by permission. All rights reserved.

All emphasis in Scripture has been added.

Some content in this book has been adapted from Jimmy Dodd's blog posts at PastorServe.

Some names and details have been changed to protect the privacy of individuals.

Edited by Matthew Boffey
Interior Design: Ragont Design
Cover Design: Kevin Richardson
Cover illustration of numeral copyright © 2019 by selim bekil / iStock (1166223765). All rights reserved.

All websites and phone numbers listed herein are accurate at the time of publication but may change in the future or cease to exist. The listing of website references and resources does not imply publisher endorsement of the site's entire contents. Groups and organizations are listed for informational purposes, and listing does not imply publisher endorsement of their activities.

Library of Congress Cataloging-in-Publication Data

Names: Dodd, Jimmy, author. | Van der Riet, Renaut, author.
Title: What great ministry leaders get right : six core competencies you need to succeed in your calling / Jimmy Dodd, Renaut van der Riet.
Description: Chicago : Moody Publishers, 2021. | Includes bibliographical references. | Summary: "Ministry throws unexpected challenges at you. What if a little more training could help you navigate them successfully? In What Great Ministry Leaders Get Right, Jimmy Dodd and Renaut van der Riet outline the six core competencies church leaders need to develop healthy, biblical, and sustainable leadership. Jimmy and Renaut address the critical lessons often missing from ministry education that all leaders need to successfully serve their congregations. Whether you've been in the pulpit for years or are just beginning your ministry education, every pastor can make sure they're prepared for the real-world challenges of ministry"-- Provided by publisher.
Identifiers: LCCN 2020035003 (print) | LCCN 2020035004 (ebook) | ISBN 9780802423139 (paperback) | ISBN 9780802499516 (ebook)
Subjects: LCSH: Christian leadership. | Church work. | Theology, Pastoral.
Classification: LCC BV652.1 .D65 2021 (print) | LCC BV652.1 (ebook) | DDC 253--dc23
LC record available at https://lccn.loc.gov/2020035003
LC ebook record available at https://lccn.loc.gov/2020035004

Originally delivered by fleets of horse-drawn wagons, the affordable paperbacks from D. L. Moody's publishing house resourced the church and served everyday people. Now, after more than 125 years of publishing and ministry, Moody Publishers' mission remains the same—even if our delivery systems have changed a bit. For more information on other books (and resources) created from a biblical perspective, go to www.moodypublishers.com or write to:

Moody Publishers
820 N. LaSalle Boulevard
Chicago, IL 60610

1 3 5 7 9 10 8 6 4 2

Printed in the United States of America

This book is dedicated to my family and to the
community of churches, pastors, staff, and church planters
around the world who have done life and ministry with
me for so many years. Through my story and what I've
written in these pages, I hope to pay forward the knowledge
and mentoring you have invested in me.

— Renaut

To PastorServe team members Wesley Horne and Wade Brown.
I am humbled by the opportunity to serve pastors
as ministry colleagues. More importantly, I am grateful that
you faithfully walk alongside me through life's labyrinth
as two of my very best friends.

— Jimmy

CONTENTS

FOREWORD

Even if I didn't know Renaut and Jimmy, I'd be honored to write the foreword for this book. It is a timely, honest, gospel-shaped overview of the commitments, rhythms, and practices of healthy ministry leaders. The need for this book, and others like it, grows exponentially, month to month.

Just this morning, a close pastor-friend shared the results of a recent survey suggesting as many as 70% of pastors are either actively seeking, or strongly considering, pursuing a vocation other than ministry. Burnout, personal failure, and depression are on the rise.

I was ordained over forty years ago, and I grieve how long it took for me to understand and practice the six core competencies discussed in this book. Let me be quick to add, don't let the word *competencies* trigger you. Renaut and Jimmy use that category to cover a wide range of health indicators.

Along with skills to develop, they stress the primacy of intimacy with God, building a culture of grace, a wholistic view of discipleship, commitments for nourishing and flourishing the people we lead, and the importance of safeguarding ourselves relationally. Such rich, rich stuff, which is more like oxygen than a great chunk of dark chocolate. I love chocolate, but oxygen is essential.

Here's a bit of my story. I came to Christ in 1968, graduated from the University of North Carolina in 1972 and Westminster Seminary in 1977. I entered vocational ministry with more passion than wisdom and more theological knowledge than emotional intelligence.

I was better at preparing sermons than taking care of my heart and was more certain of going to heaven when I died than overcoming deep shame while I lived. I made all A's in Greek and Hebrew but was clueless about conflict management, being a healthy husband and dad, and the soul-depleting demands of vocational ministry. It's no shock that I hit the wall at age fifty and had a major burnout.

By God's grace, the past twenty years have been a journey to healing, freedom, and gospel-sanity. My wife of almost forty-nine years is my best friend, I love the new rhythms of life and ministry I've built, and I have the privilege of pouring into leaders, beside me and behind me.

That brings me back to Renaut and Jimmy. As mentioned, *what* they say in this book is enough of a reason for me to commend their book. But *who* they are motivates me even more. These are men I know, love, and respect. I've seen their amazing gifts, and I've smelled their real brokenness. You'll encounter both in this book, but I get to experience both in life. And I am grateful.

They are men who carry the treasure of the gospel in their jar-of-clay-ness. That's why this book gives more hope than hype. There are scads of "how to do ministry successfully" books out there but fewer "how to live ministry life well" books.

Indeed, my friends don't present "Before and After" models of leadership. There's no "We used to be screw-ups, now we're awesome" in this book. They leave being awesome to Jesus. But there is a lot of "Join us in becoming healthier leaders and loving people well." That's why their book is more about inviting us to grace than indicting us for what we don't do well.

I've walked with Jimmy in the crucible of his commitment to bring healing, renewal, and restoration into all kinds of ministry messes and the lives of languishing leaders. I am so grateful for how God has gifted and graced my brother.

My relationship with Renaut involves both mentoring him and learning from him. His is a calling that makes my head spin and my heart dance. As impressive as Renaut's theological smarts and preaching chops are, what impacts me much more is the commitment he shares with Brooke to live out the radical implications of the gospel—in the church they lead, the family they share, and the city where they dwell. Theirs is a mercy life, a messy life, a present life—a gospel life.

It's my honor to commend both of these men to you, and their book *What Great Ministry Leaders Get Right*.

SCOTTY SMITH
Pastor Emeritus, Christ Community Church, Franklin, TN;
Teacher in Residence, West End Community Church, Nashville, TN

PREFACE

What are the baseline competencies of pastoral leadership?

PastorServe, the organization I (Jimmy) lead, took three years to personally interview hundreds of pastors in order to define the essential pastoral competencies. After initially arriving at a list of nearly one hundred, we began identifying which of them were truly critical. After follow-up interviews with pastors, we got down to fifty. Then we combined some, bringing us down to thirty. Finally, after much prayer, discussion, arguing, discussions with more pastors, and more prayer, we arrived at the PastorServe 24 Pastoral Competencies, which we've gathered under six core competencies, the outline of this book.

Since that time, the list of competencies has been used by churches around the world to form a curriculum for those serving in positions of leadership in the local church. I became aware of Renaut van der Riet using the 24 Competencies to train his leadership team at Mosaic Church in Winter Garden, Florida (unrelated to Mosaic LA). Mosaic teaches the competencies to staff, elders, deacons, and all small group leaders. When I saw how he had taken the competencies to new heights, I invited him to collaborate on this book.

While Renaut wrote chapters 1–12 and Jimmy wrote chapters 13–24 (and the stories in each of those chapters are from our individual perspectives), we have both poured ourselves into every chapter. We spent numerous days together, including a full week together in Daytona Beach, talking through each chapter in great detail and offering significant input.

This book will help you look below the layers of ministry into the deeper questions that underlie essential ministry competencies. Primarily, we unfold how the gospel enables us to live out each competency—how Jesus changes our perspective.

A big first step is simply admitting we need to learn, develop, and grow. But because fear grips so many pastors, they hesitate to tell anyone that they feel inadequate. Many carry the weight of a secret: "I am incompetent to do the job I have been called to do."

I was working with a group of Tennessee church planters when one young man broke down and began to weep. Through his tears he told the group that while he had attended a highly respected college and a well-known seminary, he felt totally incompetent in seventeen of the twenty-four competencies. He feared that if his church learned the truth about his lack of basic knowledge, he would be released. He was too fearful to confess the need, too insecure to ask for help, and too prideful to admit his incompetency. His growth in his walk with the Lord and his growth as a pastor were stunted because of his determination to pretend that he didn't need help. Sadly, that is the story of many pastors.

From Renaut

These principles and competencies have given life to me, my family, my church, and my soul. I speak from experience when I say confidently that they will do the same for you, if you will learn and apply them.

I really was not looking to write a book. In addition to ministry and community leadership roles, I am raising eight kids (a fourteen year old, two seventeen year olds, two nineteen year olds, two twenty-one year olds, and a twenty-two year old) and trying to love my wife well. Nonetheless, when Jimmy reached out to me to be a part of this project, I immediately discerned that it was important that I accept.

My only fear is that I will inadequately present these truths, such that I do not relay the importance and clarity of each of these competencies for your well-being, the well-being of those you love, and the reputation of our great God.

As you read what follows, know that I have prayed for you. As I write these very words, I feel a deep sense of urgency for the longevity of your soul, your family, and the church or ministry that you serve.

I have good reason to feel that sense of urgency in these prayers for you. We all know of the devastation that occurs when leaders crash and burn. But—good news!—it is entirely avoidable. Making progress in the twenty-four competencies in this book will help you avoid the minor and major failures of ministry, and instead steward your life, ministry, and the gospel well.

From Jimmy

The Lord led me to Renaut. I knew Mosaic Winter Garden to be a fast-growing church that was having an incredible influence on their community. When I heard that Renaut was using these competencies to train his staff, I knew we had to meet. After spending several days with Renaut over the next year, I could see that he was one of the most unique leaders I had encountered in my four decades of ministry. Renaut leads a thriving healthy church *and* leads the Axum Coffee Company, an incredible restaurant and coffee business with the goal of using profits to do good in the world—all on top of loving his wife and eight children. I suddenly felt like a sloth. After a year of talking about the competencies, we felt compelled to write this book.

Like Renaut, I am praying for you as you tackle this book. While I love the title of the book, *What Great Ministry Leaders Get Right*, it could have been called *Seminary for Dummies*. Every Bible college, seminary, and ministry training organization should teach these principles. These are the basics of leadership. They are the foundations of pastoral ministry. We pray that these competencies bring personal transformation so that you might more deeply experience the kindness of the Lord in your leadership.

INTRODUCTION

It was a moment of unanticipated crisis. I (Jimmy) sat in the church pew, squeezing my wife's hand, unsure what I would say in the next few minutes. I shot a prayer of desperation heavenward, asking the Lord for wisdom, clarity, boldness, and a godly confidence. Moments later, as I stood behind the pulpit, preparing to deliver a desperately needed word from the Lord to an overflow audience, I clearly remember the last thought that ran through my mind before I began to speak. *I must have been absent the day they covered this in seminary.*

I was blessed to attend Gordon-Conwell, one of the nation's most respected theological seminaries. I will forever be grateful for the education I received at the feet of theological giants Roger Nicole, Gordon Fee, J. I. Packer, Richard Lovelace, David Wells, and many more. However, on this particular occasion, the specific circumstance I faced was not covered in any class.

In 1992, my wife, Sally, and I had moved from Greenville, South Carolina, to Kansas City to plant a church. We had both been born and raised in Kansas and were thrilled to be going home, two children in tow. By God's grace, the church we planted began to grow, and like any church, there were days of inexpressible joy and days of gut-wrenching pain. One of the most painful days came when a young sixteen-year-old girl in our congregation was killed in a car accident. I remember going to the house to weep with her mother and stepfather as they agonized over the loss of their precious daughter, Alice.

Because her birth parents were divorced, Alice also spent a portion of her life with her birth father and stepmother, who occasionally attended another church in Kansas City. Alice's mother immediately asked me to lead the funeral service for Alice. But when the father arrived at the home, he informed Alice's mother that his pastor would be leading the funeral. So, only hours after the tragic death of their daughter, we were at a standstill. As things escalated, I stepped in and suggested that the father's pastor and I lead the service together. We could both read Scripture and share a word from the Lord and share remembrances of Alice. I assured them that I would take the lead to coordinate with the other pastor.

I had two days to connect with this man I had never met. I repeatedly called the church and his home (cell phones were rare back then) with no success. The father assured me that his pastor knew we would lead together and was prepared for his part of the service. And so, having never spoken to the pastor, I arrived at the funeral service, anticipating thirty minutes together to get acquainted, talk, and pray in a back room before we jointly ministered to an audience of nearly one thousand, the overwhelming majority of them sobbing, confused teenagers. To my dismay, the pastor arrived minutes before the service began. I had just enough time to shake hands, introduce myself, and remind him that he would speak first while I would immediately follow. We would share responsibilities at both the funeral and graveside services. I walked to the front row to sit with my wife as he began the service.

In my worst nightmare, I can't make up what came out of his

mouth. He didn't begin with a welcome. He didn't acknowledge the family or address the throng of teenagers. The very first words he spoke were, "Clearly, God lost control. This was not the plan of God. He apparently turned His back for a moment. And now, Alice has been robbed of all that was intended for her to experience. She will miss college, marriage, and parenting—all because God lost control. This was not God's plan for Alice."

I couldn't believe what I was hearing. In a couple of sentences, this pastor denied the love of God, the sovereignty of God, the providence of God, and the truth of the gospel. With close to a thousand young people in attendance, I knew that this man's message, though only five minutes long, was doing a lifetime of damage.

As I stepped up to the pulpit, God mercifully gave me the courage to begin my message with the words, "God did not lose control." A couple of people literally clapped after I said this. I went on to share a question I have often wondered about the Olympics: How can someone run a 100-meter dash in under ten seconds, while another runs for more than two hours to complete a marathon, and if they win, they both receive the same prize? The marathon runner completed an equivalent of more than four hundred 100-meter dashes! Why the same prize? Shouldn't the marathon runner be justified in receiving a medal four hundred times bigger?

The reason they receive the same prize is that they each ran the race appointed to them. Neither ran one step more or less than their race required.

Sorrowfully, Alice was not called by God to run a marathon. She was called by God to run a much shorter race. But, she ran and finished the race that the Lord had appointed for her to run. I

21

went on to tell Alice's friends and family that while Alice did unquestionably die young in a heartbreaking tragedy, she did not die prematurely. She ran into her Father's arms at the exact moment He had appointed to receive her.

The other pastor didn't stay for the graveside service. In fact, he left the building before I had completed my brief portion of the service. Following the service, dozens of teenagers stayed around to talk with my wife and I about a loving and sovereign God who desires to live in relationship with His children. What a day! What an incredible opportunity to minister under the most surreal circumstances.

Addressing the Gap

That is one of a multitude of times when I have thought to myself, *Why is there such an enormous gap between the preparation I received for ministry and real-life ministry?* And while the gap is sometimes revealed in unique circumstances, most often it is revealed in common ministry challenges. Personally, I knew I was out of my comfort zone when I was tasked with training a new group of leaders in the church, all of whom were successful businessmen, many twice my age. Or when I had to counsel others even though I was personally overwhelmed with grief following the death of my parents. I find this to be true of nearly every pastor or ministry leader: few believe they are adequately equipped for their calling. Further, the vast majority of issues that lead to the downfall of church leaders are seldom if ever discussed in training.

PastorServe has dealt with thousands of pastors who reported they were never adequately trained to confront the challenges facing them in pastoral ministry. In 1998, the Francis A. Schaeffer

Institute of Church Leadership Development continued pastoral research that had been earlier initiated by the Fuller Institute. As a part of their research, they surveyed 1,050 pastors, and 75 percent reported feeling "unqualified and/or poorly trained by their seminaries to lead and manage the church or to counsel others. This left them disheartened in their ability to pastor."[1]

While pastors appreciate courses in preaching, Christian education, and church history, for many, arriving at their first church is like being handed the keys to a small business, for which they are fundamentally unprepared. Immediately they are asked to create a budget, read a financial spreadsheet, make personnel decisions, begin a class in leadership development, mediate church conflict, or lead in crisis or tragedy. These typical pastoral demands leave pastors feeling overwhelmed, underprepared, and inadequate to face the challenges that lie before them. The result? While some weather the storm, many evacuate.

I have talked with seminary presidents who readily agree that their institution lacks baseline pastoral competency training. And yet, they sadly report that there is little hope for change, as adding basic pastoral competency courses to the curriculum means eliminating an equal number of existing courses. And precious few departments and professors (particularly those with tenure) are prepared to place their specialized fields of study on the chopping block. I applaud alternative forms of pastoral education that address real-life pastoral ministry, often requiring students to serve in local church settings throughout their educational training.

This book addresses some of what gets missed in seminary. But since a book or even a class are in themselves insufficient, we encourage you to read this book in community. The contents will be most readily absorbed and applied in the context of a church staff, ministry leadership team, or local cohort of leaders. Toward that end, we encourage you to discuss together the reflection questions included at the end of each chapter. May the Lord encourage you as you dive into these ministry competencies together.

PART I

Care for Your Soul (Vertical Foundations)

CHAPTER 1

PRAYER AND FASTING

By the mid twenty-teens, Central Florida had been shaken by a string of pastoral failures. In 2011, a prominent ministry leader from our area was found dead of a drug overdose. Between 2012 and 2013, three more prominent pastors had affairs, one committing suicide shortly after. It was devastating.

Almost instantly, the pastoral team at my church began to wrestle with the realities around this type of fall. We engaged in an ongoing conversation about how to keep each other out of the shadows. It was both encouraging and deeply practical.

Then just before Easter in 2014 I got a text from Joel, one of the other teaching pastors at my church. "Another pastor went down," it said. I could tell he was brokenhearted.

I had met this latest leader recently at a conference where he was speaking. The topic? The importance of stability in marriage. It was painful to hear this news after he had ministered to my own marriage only months before.

A *Christianity Today* writer observed that while the Christian press speculated that "the recent trend is the spirit of Jezebel . . . picking off pastors one by one as they succumb to the evil desires in their own hearts, David Swanson, senior pastor of First Presbyterian

Church of Orlando, told the *Orlando Sentinel* that it's probably more related to the feelings of isolation experienced by large-church leaders."[2] While it may be worse for leaders of large churches, isolation is common to virtually all pastors.

As the leader of a church, I was stunned by this assessment. It woke me up. Is it inevitable that I am going to steal, become addicted, or have an affair? If so, I was prepared to quit ministry. There's no way I wanted that story to be my story.

Developing Intimacy

I wondered what was missing in the lives of these leaders to create the space that allows anyone to make such devastating decisions. My first assumption was a lack of accountability; these guys were probably lone leaders who didn't answer to anyone. However, my assumption was off. These pastors had solid accountability parameters in place. The trouble was that over time they started actively hiding the truth.

As my ministry team and I continued to explore this problem in our profession, we found that these leaders cultivated an environment for deception. They became more and more isolated and less and less connected to key people in their lives, starting with God. This disconnection caused a deep lack of intimacy. And in this breakdown of intimacy, we began to discover the key. This is how you will not fall, how you will not destroy your life and your family, how you will not embarrass yourself and your congregation: You need intimacy.

When we are in love with the God who created us and in love with our spouse and in love with our biblical community— when we are intimate with them—there are no giant, devastating decisions we will make. We simply don't make those kinds of decisions when we are deeply connected with these key relationships.

When it comes to developing intimacy with God, my team and I have found that nothing compares to the spiritual disciplines of prayer and fasting. Prayer and fasting are key practices that solicit God to move in us, through us, and around us. In biblical history, prayer and fasting saved a nation from genocide (Esth. 4:16) and brought life-saving clarity and wisdom (Ex. 34:28; Dan. 10:2–3). They have also been integral to revivals throughout church history. When we incorporate prayer and fasting into our regular practice, they remind us that ministry must be done with God's power and intervention. They keep us at the feet of Jesus instead of trusting in our own strength to transform others. These are reasons enough to practice prayer and fasting, but there is something even deeper in these two competencies that keep us safe and free.

In our obsession to produce fruit and be "good and faithful servants," producing something worthy that will have a lasting legacy, many have neglected the inner life. William Carey, Joshua Marshman, and William Ward wrote, "Prayer, secret, fervent, believing prayer, lies at the root of all personal godliness."[3] As leaders desiring to remain faithful to Jesus, the most important skill is keeping our soul. Many, if not most, of us struggle mightily in this. It's no wonder so many ministry leaders strive to create outward success while simultaneously constructing inward disasters. So often our eyes are fixed on whatever our church culture deems ministry success, when our prize should be the surpassing greatness of knowing Christ.

The Power and Purpose of Prayer

Years ago, I encountered a statement about prayer that has haunted me ever since. It has become a window into my own soul. Richard

Foster, in his classic book *Celebration of Discipline*, writes, "To pray is to change. Prayer is the central avenue God uses to transform us. If we are unwilling to change, we will abandon prayer as a noticeable characteristic of our lives."[4] Foster's insight into prayer launched me into a personal journey of understanding the power and purpose of prayer beyond anything I could imagine.

I have discovered that a life submitted to Christ results in my soul desiring to be more like His. By the same token, a soul submitted to no one desires no change at all. In fact, a person obsessed with self, openly or secretly, resists change. The more I am submitted to Christ, the more deeply I desire change. The more deeply I desire change, the more consistent and authentic my personal, private prayer life becomes. As Foster suggests, prayer is a natural by-product of the heart that desires to be shaped by God's transforming work. So, my personal, private prayer life is a direct reflection of my inner desire to change and become more like Jesus. Stated another way, my personal prayer reveals how much I really want my life to be about Jesus.

When my prayer life becomes inconsistent or inauthentic, it immediately alerts me that something deep within my soul has shifted from being captivated by Jesus to being captivated by something else. Consistency in prayer is the gift for detecting soul erosion early.

Prayer is both a thermometer and a remedy. It is a thermometer in that its absence from our lives reflects deeper things about passion, intimacy, and trust. A prayerless life reveals that our eyes are fixed on the wrong prize. Prayer is also a remedy in that it reconnects us to the gospel and catapults us back into God's world, God's heart, and God's love. Prayer safeguards our lives, our families, the church, and the gospel.

Prayer allows us to stay close to God. While God's work is to do in us and through us whatever He sees fit, prayer is our work. We remain ever present on the spiritual frontier, and God handles the rest.

Participating in our own sanctification is one of the great privileges of every believer. Incredibly, the Lord promises to finish the work in us, while at the same time inviting us to participate in our sanctification. We have all the privilege of participation, yet the ultimate responsibility to make it happen lies with the Lord. It's almost identical to the idea that if we are interested in what God will do in our lives, all we need to do is pray. If we have a consistent and authentic prayer life with God, He gives us insight into our lives. Isn't that crazy? He gives us the answers! We get to be an active participant in our own beautiful life journey.

> Being competent in prayer and fasting is far less about soliciting God to do things for us and far more about placing ourselves in the soil where God does things in us.

Foster says, "A farmer is helpless to grow grain; all he can do is provide the right conditions for the growing of grain. . . . The Disciplines are God's way of getting us into the ground."[5]

Being competent in prayer and fasting is far less about soliciting God to do things for us and far more about placing ourselves in the soil where God does things in us. It is far less about asking God to do things for us and far more about revealing what is in us and asking Him to transform us. It is learning to dare the soul to believe the things God has already said and done and to submit to His renewing work.

This is why prayer and fasting are essential for any ministry leader. The presence or absence of our authentic, private, personal prayer and fasting lives is a thermometer displaying the heat of our intimacy with God. This is a must for anyone who seeks to have longevity in authentic gospel ministry. And this is where the true beauty of fasting becomes the companion to prayer in keeping our souls.

Reclaiming Fasting

Fasting is the most misunderstood of the spiritual disciplines. Many of us resist the discipline of fasting. And still more of us believe it's just a tool we use to solicit something from the Almighty God of the universe. But actually, fasting is another means of sanctification. Fasting is a gift through which we can see clearly the idols hiding deep within our heart.

Richard Foster writes:

> More than any other Discipline, fasting reveals the things that control us. . . . We cover up what is inside us with food and other good things, but in fasting these things surface. . . . Anger, bitterness, jealousy, strife, fear—if they are within us, they will surface during fasting. . . . We can rejoice in this knowledge because we know that healing is available through the power of Christ.[6]

Fasting teaches our souls to trust God and His story rather than trusting ourselves and our stories. It is a discipline that teaches the soul to believe in God, reveals our unbelief, and invites us to engage with God in prayer so that His transforming power might reveal the way to freedom and produce the healing we need.

This is where our true journey begins as pastors and church

leaders. It does not begin and end with learning the skills of outward ministry but with the skills of soul keeping, of life living, of making the gospel beautiful inside ourselves. This internal work must happen long before we try to make it beautiful outside ourselves. We must learn the skill of spiritual discipline first, for it leads to a life-giving intimacy with our Creator, the burning center of ministry.

The Gift That Keeps Our Souls Well

Often we see ministry obstacles as our greatest challenges: the management of people, the skills to lead, the structures, strategies and plans to grow, the conflicts to resolve, and on and on. According to Scripture, however, our greatest challenge is in fact a spiritual war that is raging, one in which the enemy is extremely competent and unrelenting. We often think that the enemy is working to try and tempt us and derail our behavior so that we will be ineffective and feel guilty and shamed. The Scripture paints a much darker picture. The enemy does not care about these things. The enemy cares that you are dead—spiritually dead, physically dead, emotionally dead, dead to the gospel, dead to God, dead to life and freedom, dead to belief. He wants our families dead. He wants the church dead. He hates God, he hates you, and he hates me. This is war. Guarding our inner life is our single greatest responsibility.

You can begin to see how fasting and prayer are such gifts to us to keep our souls well. It is in the practice of prayer and fasting that we plant ourselves deeply in the soil in which God transforms us into His likeness. If we are to be leaders sustained in life and ministry in a manner worthy of our calling, we must constantly inhabit the spaces where God transforms us into His likeness. This is very likely our greatest work as church leaders. It is not to lead others but to be led by Jesus. Then, and only then, will we actually be equipped to lead others.

As new pastors enter ministry, their problems are not limited to a lack of ministry competency but an inexperience in achieving personal holiness through secret, fervent, believing prayer. Without it, they are vulnerable to failure.

Prayer and fasting are not what we do to get our work done. They are our work. Yes, prayer and fasting may solicit God's provision, but more importantly they produce intimacy with God. You may not get what you want, but you will get what you need: a reminder that your soul needs God. And if He grants what you ask, well, that is secondary.

Prayer and fasting are critical skills to master as a church leader. If we neglect them, we will certainly cultivate a space where intimacy dissolves. Once that space is created, the enemy who wants us dead will most certainly move in. And we will most certainly begin to make devastating choices that hurt our congregation and destroy our families.

Be the church leader who does not fall, but instead stands strong, like a tree planted by streams of living water (Ps. 1:3). Set yourself up to defy the odds.

SELF-ASSESSMENT

On a scale of 1 to 5, how developed are you in the competency of prayer and fasting?

1	2	3	4	5
"I admit I am clueless in this competency."	"I know enough to know what I don't know."	"I can get by."	"I have a healthy skill set in this competency."	"I'm killing it in this area."

CHAPTER 2

CHRIST-CENTERED WORSHIP

One Sunday night when our church was new and very small, I preached one of those messages that was everything I wanted a message to be. And yet I was frustrated. We had seventeen people in a room that seated 250. The room was so big that it felt more like three. I remember driving home that night frustrated that we had brought this amazing message and worship to the table and only seventeen people experienced it.

As I was driving home, I remember saying, "Look God, I get that numbers don't matter, but really, seventeen?" I didn't expect anything. I was just venting a bit. But God almost tangibly said, "Pull over. We need to talk."

I physically pulled over on the side of the road to wrestle with God on this thought. God was saying to me, "Who are you really doing this for?" *Well, that's obvious. I'm doing this for you, Lord.* But I realized God was challenging me. If I'm really doing this for God, then what difference does it make if there are seventeen, seven hundred, or seven thousand people present? I realized then that though I claimed to do these things for God, that wasn't completely true. The breadth of my preaching influence mattered greatly to me, and I measured whether my effort was worth it or not based on how many people showed up. I sat there on the side of that road and asked God to help me move my focus and the motive for my efforts; I promised God and myself that whether there were two people or one hundred thousand, I would get up and preach with the same vigor and passion, because it would be for Him and Him alone. I did not realize it then, but my understanding of worship, deep, Christ-centered worship, was beginning to form.

From Life Categories to All of Life

That experience has shaped tremendously how I minister. More importantly, it has shaped how I live. It triggered a journey of exploring what it meant to live all of life as worship. I realized that I had separated my life into categories of activity. Some of my life was active work for God, some active worship of God, some common and neutral, and some a struggle. Worship (praying, singing, meditating) was just one category, lumped in with eliminating the worship of other things. In fact, my life paralleled how many churches talk about the worship service. We divide our gatherings into parts: the welcome, the worship, the teaching, the announcements, the closing. Worship is just one component. All of this misses the deep and wonderful reality of what Christ-centered worship really is, individually and corporately. The truth is, every moment is worship.

God's vision for true worship has been revealed all along in Scripture. In the Old Testament, there is a beautiful word that captures this idea of life being worship so eloquently: *avodah*. *Avodah* is a Hebrew word that means "work," "service," and "worship."[7] In Exodus 34:21, Moses is renewing the covenant when God says,

"Six days you shall work [avodah]." In Psalm 104:23, we read, "Then man goes out to his work [avodah], and to his labor until evening." In the Scriptures, *avodah* describes the backbreaking work of making bricks in Egypt and the craftsmanship of the artists building the Tabernacle.

In other passages, the emphasis is on worship. Joshua 24:15 says, "But as for me and my house, we will serve [avodah] the LORD." Exodus 8:1 carries the sense of worship: "This is what the LORD says: Let my people go, so that they may worship [avodah] me" (NIV). *Avodah* describes the work of the Levites and priests leading the people in worship.

This word reminds us that God is an efficient God who does not ask us to work and then worship. Rather, He tells us to do both concurrently and faithfully. God's plan is for our work and worship to blend seamlessly in our lives. God intends for our work, our vocation, our calling to be an act of God-honoring worship. God never intended for us to compartmentalize our lives into work and worship. Life is the work of worship.

Romans 12 confirms this understanding of worship as the umbrella over all Christian activity. The apostle Paul writes, "Therefore, I urge you, brothers and sisters, in view of God's mercy [referring to the gospel], to offer your bodies as a living sacrifice, holy and pleasing to God" (NIV). This calls us to give our all, our every moment, our whole life. Then Paul adds something absolutely exceptional: "This is your true and proper worship." This single statement changes everything about the way we should understand worship.

Building on the Old Testament concept of *avodah*, Paul affirms that worship is an everyday, moment-by-moment, all-encompassing way in which we live our lives. My worship is what

I'm doing right now. When I drive home. When I respond to my kids. When I don't respond well and have to repent. Worship is my continual, constant, nonstop desire to have everything I do show the gospel to be beautiful and bring honor to Christ. When it's my obsession to reflect Jesus in every circumstance, that becomes *Christ*-centered worship. This is the worship Paul is guiding us to live out. Christ-centered worship is the deliberate process of directing my thinking and asking regularly, in every moment, what is my opportunity to glorify God?

So then, what does this mean when we preach to a gathering of seventeen in a room built for 250? Instead of showing up for them, we show up for God. Our motivating factor is that this is precisely what we were made for. Every action has the same goal: worship Christ. Worshiping on Sunday is now in essence no different than walking down the road on a Tuesday or enjoying a quiet moment of reflection or talking to my teenager on about homework or wrestling through a tense moment with my spouse. Every opportunity is an equal opportunity to engage in active worship.

So, if worship is our response to God's mercy, and if it is the work (avodah) of our whole life, then what exactly is our life's work? Is it ministry? Is it vocation? Is it family? Yes, yes, and yes. Our life's work, our worship, our *avodah*, is from sunup to sundown. It is the keeping of your children, your spouse, the ministry you are privileged to lead. It encompasses your soul, your body, your mind, your friendships. It covers your calendar, your grocery shopping, your naps. What would it look like if, at the moment we open our eyes each morning, we chose the mindset that everything we are about to do is an act of worship? The reality is, if we aren't worshiping Christ in everything we do, we are robbing not only God of glory but ourselves of the story God has for us. Our active practice of spiritual worship is giving ourselves to the greater story of God.

Tremendous Benefit

Living a life centered on Christ is a biblical mandate, and this is certainly enough reason to do it. However, in God's kindness, it has tremendous benefits for how we lead and shepherd.

To begin with, the greatest freedom in preaching the Word of God comes when what you preach is what you live. If I'm living my life in pursuit of knowing God, if I am studying Scripture as much for personal edification as for the Sunday sermon, if I share my life with my neighbors, if I live in the local and global community—basically doing all the things I'm asking everyone else to do—then my preaching will be born out of my life. My preaching is an outcome of living my life before an audience of one. It becomes that simple. That is such a tremendous freedom. It eliminates hiddenness and creates vulnerability, which is so very helpful to our people.

Secondly, you get to lead how the Bible calls you to lead. You are no longer a detached leader trying to bring others where you have not gone. Now you are a leader being led, one who says, "I am following Jesus, and I'm sharing my journey so you can follow Him as I follow Him." With this conviction, your significance and success have little to do with whether you are growing a church and keeping people. You are living life with eyes fixed on Jesus and sharing with people so they can follow Him with you. Whether they follow you as you follow Jesus or not, you still live out your God-given purpose to know Him and make Him known.

Finally, while all Christ followers have the benefit of living an authentic, vulnerable life following Jesus, we leaders get the added benefit of bringing our whole lives to the frontstage so people who see us experience His Word in our life. Some people see this in negative terms: living in a fishbowl. I do not. Light and vulnerability is our friend, and everyone seeing our lives in all of their beauty and brutality is a gift. For one, it creates a tremendous connection between us and God and sparks a desire from others to follow Jesus as well. Second, it helps us experience freedom and transformation.

For the church leader, worship is critical. Christ-centered worship keeps the soul well. It protects our soul from the erosion of idolatry and hypocrisy. It allows us to behave and speak and authentically believe in the gospel—in all of the gospel. This is how we are to live.

SELF-ASSESSMENT

On a scale of 1 to 5, how developed are you in the competency of Christ-centered worship?

1	2	3	4	5
"I admit I am clueless in this competency."	"I know enough to know what I don't know."	"I can get by."	"I have a healthy skill set in this competency."	"I'm killing it in this area."

CHAPTER 3

DOCTRINAL SOUNDNESS

Although I have always known that a basic understanding of doctrine was important, early on in ministry I found it safer to stick to the basics. Anything beyond that seemed to polarize people, especially in youth ministry and in my formative years in a more attractional church model. And yet, as I matured in life and ministry, I became more and more captivated by the wonder of God's revealed Word. I discovered the beauty of wrestling with the Scriptures and clarifying and articulating what discoveries I was making. The deeper I dug into the Scriptures, the more I began to realize how many things I had said or taught out of a lack of understanding. I began to realize that I had all too often made assumptions about what the Scriptures meant. I came to understand the overwhelming responsibility to have a real handle on doctrine.

Holy Fear

God extends an invitation and challenge to all believers to know and understand the depths of His revealed Word. But for those of us who teach, it is far more than an invitation. It is a heavy responsibility, one that should lead to holy fear!

In the early New Testament church, before the Gentile world was integrated into the body of believers, James wrote an instructive letter to the believers scattered throughout the Roman Empire. The letter had two purposes: to encourage believers to stand firm in the midst of seemingly insurmountable odds and to instruct a body of believers unsure about how to live as Christians. In this context, James wrote, "Not many of you should become teachers, my brothers, for you know that we who teach will be judged with greater strictness" (James 3:1). God sets the bar extremely high for those who endeavor to teach or preach because people follow us. Therefore, we are held to a higher standard; we are expected to have a clear understanding of what we teach.

James's admonition to teachers is sobering. However, there is a greater teacher who tells us to uphold good doctrine. Jesus addresses the weight of the responsibility to teach when He reflects on someone leading His children astray: "But whoever causes one of these little ones who believe in me to sin, it would be better for him to have a great millstone fastened around his neck and to be drowned in the depth of the sea" (Matt. 18:6). While the context of this warning is not specifically preaching, we know that one place that holds potential to lead God's children astray is teaching and preaching. Because we are teachers and preachers, people assume we know what we are talking about, and sadly, they often buy in without question (unlike the Bereans in Acts 17:11). If we lead God's children astray, the Lord says we would be better off drowned. This is not subtle or gentle; it should scare the living daylights out of us.

At Mosaic Church, we have several young leaders who gather

weekly to be trained in the craft of preaching. Part of the training involves practicing preaching. Following the sermons, we critique and offer constructive criticism. Almost every week, I remind them that if they have not studied the context and the deeper theological, doctrinal, and gospel implications of the passage, they are likely to lead someone astray. And, if they lead someone astray, they have it coming.

But what about grace? Don't get me wrong; I know we will all make mistakes in our teaching. God's grace for our weakness is awesome, and His patience for our limitations is astounding. However, if we make those mistakes because we are unwilling to do the hard work of exploring doctrine and theology, then it is not our limitations that are the problem but our fears and our laziness.

It is this truth that drove the leadership of Mosaic Church to significantly intensify the process for nominating, training, and confirming our elders. (See chapter 16 on leadership development.) Nominees undergo a rigorous two-year process that includes the reading of about twenty-five books, including a systematic theology tome about five inches thick. We painstakingly go through the book chapter by chapter during the first year. We do this because anyone who endeavors to shepherd and teach in a biblical context had better know the details of doctrine. We are saving them from the rope and the big rock!

Doctrinal Balance

A sound grasp on doctrine is a crucial competency for any ministry leader. Yet I understand why doctrine is often seen as a can of worms, or why we want to keep it simple. Many leaders prefer to stay in the shallows, borrowing simple mainline evangelical doctrinal statements rather than diving deep, where controversy lurks. We've witnessed the battles between Calvinism and Arminianism. We've seen friendships dissolve over theology. We have seen churches or whole denominations split over theological differences. As a result, many conclude that doctrine is both decisive and divisive. They may declare, "Wouldn't it be easier if we agreed to stick to the foundational story, to keep it simple? Jesus Christ came, died, rose again, and is coming again. That's all we need to know. The rest just leads to trouble." But keeping it theologically simple is not so simple a proposition.

Here's our dilemma. As biblical teachers, we simply don't have the luxury of having only a basic understanding of doctrine or a shallow knowledge of biblical truth. We must be able to do a deep dive into the Scriptures, especially so that we can help people face the complexities of life with godly wisdom. Furthermore, we need to know which hills we should be willing to die on and which ones we'd be fools to die on.

Picture your hands, the left closed and the right open. In your left hand are beliefs that most Christians agree are primary: Jesus Christ is God, the Bible is His inspired Word, Jesus is the only way of salvation, we are saved by grace through faith, and so on. We close this hand. We will give our lives for these primary biblical truths. In your right hand are secondary issues, such as believer's baptism, form of church government, eschatology, the practice of spiritual gifts, style of worship, and other similar topics. For every topic I hold in my open right hand, there are smart people who love Jesus on both sides of the issue. Problems surface when we take something from the secondary right hand and place it in our primary left hand.

That said, we must have a robust understanding of what

we hold in our left hand. When we don't, we run the real risk of making assumptions about God's Word and what it says. We will then, at best, teach inaccurately. We may even dumb down our theology to omit anything that might offend. At worst, we may teach and preach heresy. Conversely, none of us can be as astute as a seminary professor on every topic in Scripture. We feel overwhelmed with the thought of mastering even closed-hand doctrines!

This tension is right and good. Think of it in terms of how we experience one another daily. When we encounter each other, we really only see the surface: our skin, hair, and face. Everything below that—our veins, our skeleton, our muscles, our organs—are hidden from sight.

Now imagine if I greeted you as just my skeleton. Most likely, you would scream, run away, and have nightmares for the rest of your life. Though vital, our skeletons were not meant to be front and center. They were meant to lend support.

On the other hand, what if we removed my skeleton? Without the skeletal structure, nothing would function correctly. Movement in my face, my hands, my legs—all would be gone. I would be a big blob flopping around. The skeletal structure is what gives my flesh form and function. Without the skeleton, the flesh is useless.

This biological dynamic is the same when we consider doctrine and the narrative of Scripture. The narrative is the beautiful and relatable form in which God communicated all of His principles and truths. In Jesus, we see the Word made the flesh (John 1:1, 14). Doctrine is the function and form onto which the narrative is built.

Here is the challenge for those who teach: If we primarily study doctrine (the skeleton) while marginalizing the narrative (the flesh), if we become obsessed with rightness and preach doctrine rather than preaching Jesus, it will become inaccessible, uncomfortable, and, frankly, intellectually scary. When teachers become obsessed with preaching doctrine, there are two common outcomes: people either become captivated with being theologically right or sink into theological ambiguity and comfort, leaving for a more comfortable church with more relatable preaching.

On the other hand, if we ignore doctrine, preaching only the narrative of Scripture (and even then, only the comfortable parts) through our own way of thinking, we simply end up with our own philosophies. Chances are, we will have a very comfortable preaching style and message but will lead our congregation astray.

Balance is key. The essential role the skeleton plays in the well-being of our bodies was heightened for me recently when one of my friends needed a bone marrow transplant. I learned that the skeleton is the primary organ in the immune system; without the skeleton, there is essentially no immune system. In fact, after a patient has a bone marrow transplant, hospital staffs refer to them as the "walking dead," because nearly their entire immune system has been eliminated. When we remove doctrine, we remove the immune system from the narrative of the gospel. We are left with just our limited thinking and impulses, compromised constantly. This is the great nightmare.

Guard the Right Thing

Our calling is not to get doctrine right for its own sake. Our calling is to guard the beauty and truth of the gospel. We guard the gospel, not the doctrine.

In my early years, I had a handle on the narrative of the gospel:

creation, fall, rescue, restoration. However, I had little real concept of the doctrine of the gospel, understanding the process by which God brings us to Himself and makes us right with Him. Regeneration, justification, restoration, glorification, and the order in which these realities take place change so much of our understanding of grace and mercy. These deeper things I did not know well.

Every doctrine in Scripture ultimately points the reader to grace in Jesus Christ. Unquestionably, there are doctrines that initially appear unrelated to the larger story of the gospel. And yet, each of these theological truths has a significant impact on our understanding of the gospel.

Take the question of whether God chooses us or we choose God. This is not a matter of eternity, because either way, we belong to Jesus. However, it does deeply influence how we experience God's grace and mercy.

I learned this lesson firsthand. When my wife and I decided to pursue the adoption of our four children from Ethiopia, we did not check in with them to ask if they wanted to be adopted. We did not feel compelled to present them our story to see if they liked us, and we did not share with them all the ways we would make their lives better if they chose us. We paid all the money, did all the traveling, filled out all the paperwork, did all the work, went and got them, and brought them home. We wrestled through the transition with them. We walked through the trauma of their past and all the things they lost when they came to a new family in the United States. They did not choose us; we chose them.

Do you see how deep doctrinal issues do touch on the gospel? Though it matters where we land on them, what matters more is how our position influences our witness and experience of the gospel. As a teacher or preacher, you better know where you stand

and why you stand there, especially as it relates to matters of eternity but also for areas of conviction and matters of opinion. What we believe, whether we are intentional about that belief or simply unaware of it, shapes what we teach and how we pastor.

This became abundantly clear to me in the process we went through as a church a few years ago. We were in the process of searching for a new student ministries pastor. We sorted through hundreds of résumés, finally narrowing it down to just a few. First, we conducted phone interviews to confirm that the candidates clearly understood our particular theological positions. Then we brought the final candidates to our church for face-to-face visits and asked them to preach to our students. Without exception, each preached motives and applications inconsistent with what they said they believed about our particular theological position. In this case, they affirmed a Reformed perspective but preached an Arminian one. More troubling was that not one of them comprehended they were violating the very truths they affirmed they believed. To a person, the doctrinal beliefs they articulated lacked the depth and richness of the gospel. During the phone interview, they embraced what they had read on our website. What they really believed bled out when they preached. The same is true for us.

SELF-ASSESSMENT

On a scale of 1 to 5, how developed are you in the competency of doctrinal soundness?

1	2	3	4	5
"I admit I am clueless in this competency."	"I know enough to know what I don't know."	"I can get by."	"I have a healthy skill set in this competency."	"I'm killing it in this area."

CHAPTER 4

SUFFERING AND WEAKNESS

We live in a fascinating, audacious, prosperous culture in America. America was founded on the premise of equality and freedom. Our founding fathers declared this in the Declaration of Independence when they said we had a right to pursue happiness. As we pursue this and other supposedly self-evident rights, we discover *happiness* and *equality* can mean very different things to different people. For example, we assume that since all are equal, anyone can become anything they want. (Sadly, systemic racism has disproved this assumption. See chapter 23.) We believe that we must eliminate our weaknesses and develop our strengths until we are strong, self-sufficient, and able. We also tend to equate happiness with maximal comfort and convenience. We do not mind working hard and struggling for a season, as long as it leads us to luxury.

The result of this is a culture where we conclude that suffering should be avoided at all costs and that anything that causes ongoing suffering can't be good, right, or of God. Additionally, we believe that any weakness in us must be either eliminated or minimized, certainly not embraced.

But this is simply not the gospel.

In our Western, sanitized version of Christianity, we secretly believe that if God calls us into something, He is obligated to make it go smoothly. If it remains hard, then God must not be in it, and we must have made a mistake. This is not a biblical view of God's call to mission. Just look at the lives of the early followers of Jesus. Based on their experience alone, I would say that until you can honestly scream, "I'm over missional living!" you haven't really begun to live on mission.

My own experience has also confirmed that missional life can be simultaneously rooted in God's will and deeply challenging. In January of 2009, my wife and I discovered a little five-year-old orphan girl in Ethiopia who captured our hearts. We sensed a clear call to bring her home to our family. At the time, my wife and I had four beautiful biological children between the ages of two and nine. Over the next three long years, we discovered two very important things. One, the process to adopt is very tedious, difficult, and emotional. Two, our little orphan girl had three older siblings. Before I write the next part, I should say, "Don't try this at home! It's very dangerous and unwise unless you have deep clarity on your calling from God." Long story very short, God invited us to adopt all four.

> In our Western, sanitized version of Christianity, we secretly believe that if God calls us into something, He is obligated to make it go smoothly.

We were not naïve as we walked into this story. We knew this was going to be very, very hard. In 2013, we were eighteen months into the journey with our new family. Nothing was left of our former life. My wife is an introvert and a perfectionist.

You'd never think it because she is very outgoing and compassionate, but she thrives in environments that are quiet and organized. She deeply dislikes ongoing noise and chaos. Our new life was in many ways her nightmare. She lost her life for the sake of Christ. About six months after our adopted children arrived, my wife declared through tears, "I'm over missional living!" God had brought us into a new season of life, a season filled with challenge, struggle, heartache, and suffering. And I wouldn't trade it for the world!

Today, we have grieved many losses and continue to struggle under the weight of our new reality. Just a few nights ago, my wife declared once again, "I can't do this anymore!" This is not the first time, nor will it be the last, that she or I declare these words. These moments come and go, but they are very real. It breaks my heart when I see my wife and children struggle under the weight of missional life. I don't have many words to make it all okay. So, I fall back on the only thing that makes any sense of all this insanity: the raw reality of the gospel of Jesus.

The Work of Redemption Is Seldom Pretty

Ministry is the work of redemption, and the work is hard. Philippians 2 tells us that Jesus emptied Himself, setting His rights aside to come to earth to rescue us. He takes on the form of a servant. He confronts darkness, lies, idols, self-righteousness, and death, all while bringing comfort to the weak, scared, lonely, lost, and broken. All this comes at a great cost. He pours Himself out in proclaiming and displaying the values and wisdom of the kingdom, and He has a front-row seat as people fail Him time and time again with their selfishness, idols, and pettiness. In spite of the challenges, some miraculous and beautiful stories emerge.

Of course, Jesus pours Himself out to the extreme—He gives Himself over to death at the hands of those whom He came to save. Jesus dies a horrid death, both physically and spiritually.

His work of redemption is beautiful. The process of redemption is incredibly hard. God literally tears Himself apart to rescue us. The triune God is broken into pieces for us.

Jesus tells His followers to expect to suffer like Him. "Pick up your cross and follow me." Considering Jesus' life, I do not believe we should see these crosses simply as the natural struggles we go through on planet Earth. Yes, those struggles are part of our journey here, just as Jesus struggled throughout His life. However, His cross was the means to our redemption, the intentional and voluntary act of suffering and dying to rescue us. Throughout our lives, we will consistently be asked to take up the burdens and sins of others to be the redemptive ambassadors of Jesus. When we take up the suffering of others or suffer for righteousness' sake, we are carrying our cross.

Picking up our cross often looks like setting our rights aside to rescue others. We become like a servant, seeing all circumstances, resources, and relationships as a means to serve Christ, while demonstrating and declaring the gospel. We confront darkness, lies, idols, self-righteousness, and death (especially within ourselves) while bringing comfort to the weak, scared, lonely, lost, and broken.

All this will come at great cost to us. We pour ourselves out in proclaiming and displaying the values and wisdom of the kingdom. We watch as the people we serve fail us time and time again. We put our hearts and bodies on the line, and when people reject or abandon us, it feels like being broken into pieces. Sound familiar?

In spite of the challenges, some miraculous and beautiful stories emerge. If we will follow Jesus and take up our crosses and live as He did, then we will see much of our labor and sacrifice and death resurrected. We will see a more powerful and glorified version of our stories, our lives, our dreams, and our hopes than anything we could have imagined. We will see some of those we poured into rise up and follow in our footsteps and live redemptive lives. Despite what the world believes, beauty is wrapped up in suffering. Somehow, life is the fruit of death.

Our Greatest Weakness

The gospel also frees us to embrace weakness. This is one of our beautiful privileges as Christ followers.

When we embrace redemptive living, it will reveal in us our deepest and darkest depravity. It will stir up our long-buried dysfunctions and brokenness and reveal our weaknesses with extraordinary clarity. Doesn't that sound wonderful? No. Why not? Because we have been raised up to eliminate, minimize, bury, or hide our weaknesses, not put them front and center. Yet in God's paradigm, they become our gift.

Perhaps the most well-known biblical example of this truth is Paul's thorn in the flesh. Paul is discussing his endurance and hardships in ministry when he writes, "A thorn was given me in the flesh, a messenger of Satan to harass me, to keep me from becoming conceited. Three times I pleaded with the Lord about this, that it should leave me" (2 Cor. 12:7–8). This thorn profoundly impacted Paul's life. Even though he had a tough exterior, he was weak. We all have the experience of struggling with something hard. For some, it might be debilitating migraines. For others, it may be depression. Depression comes and goes as it pleases. And when it hits hard, you don't want to do anything. You beg God to take it away. Paul's thorn may have been a demonic presence that hounded him. Whatever it was, it was clearly difficult. He begged God to take it away. God didn't. Whatever the thorn, God kept it in, and it made Paul feel weak and small. Then God reveals to Paul the power and purpose of weakness. He says directly to Paul, "My grace is sufficient for you, for my power is made perfect in weakness" (2 Cor. 12:9).

Read that verse again carefully.

Like you, I used to assume that this verse promises that when I am weak, God will be made perfect and show Himself strong *by making me strong*. But that is not what it says. God says that *in* my weakness God's power will be made perfect. Essentially, He is saying my weakness is the reality that makes His power evident and perfect. How? Because in my weakness I will remain mindful of who He is and who I am. In my weakness I will posture myself in Christ and His story and find joy in the privilege of participating despite my weakness, rather than be discouraged that my weakness means I'm a failure. It will keep me from believing I did something with God's help, when in reality He did something while allowing me to help. It frees me from the need to be the hero. Our culture tells us that our greatest strength is self-reliance and that self-doubt is our enemy. In fact, the opposite is true. The greatest danger to my soul is self-reliance. My safest place is reliance on God.

We are limited, and God is limitless. We are weak, and God is strong. We are dependent, and God is dependable. We are human, and God is divine. And yet, the eternal is connected to the temporal as weak human beings are invited to participate in God's story. God does not participate in our story by giving us a bit of extra strength. We participate in His story without fear because He already knows our limitations. We can embrace our weakness and enjoy our strengths simultaneously, since both are part of God's grace toward us.

Like many of you, living a missional life regularly reveals my weakness and limitations, making me feel as if I have failed God. The story that has most freed me is the story of Peter denying Christ. Just hours after Peter declares he would never abandon Jesus, he denies Him three times—in Jesus' most vulnerable moment.

I will not know the pain of the moment right after the rooster crowed and Peter realized what he had done, but I'm quite confident that everything he knew of himself was gone in an instant.

Here's what I've come to discover: If Peter's actions were no surprise to Jesus, neither are my weaknesses. Jesus anticipates my weakness every time I am on mission for Him. The key is that Peter is in the courtyard, instead of hiding behind a door somewhere with the other guys. The point is not that Peter denied Christ but that Peter dared to step into the courtyard. When we step into hard things to participate in redemption on behalf of Christ, we will at times fail. But failing as I pursue the mission God has set before me is far better than hiding behind a white picket fence and a comfortable life. And even in failure, God is redeeming all things for our ultimate good and His ultimate glory (Rom. 8:28).

I've needed that sermon every day for the last several years. I've needed it since I've encountered the beautiful collision of my family that grew our numbers from four to eight children. I know Jimmy and his wife, Sally, have experienced pain as they adopted and grew their family from three children to five. I have stared into weaker places of my heart that I didn't know could even exist, places that I would have equated with evil people. I have stood in moments in front of a child, biological or adopted, where all I could find was frustration and hatefulness. I've wondered how a human can feel and think these things about their very own child that I have felt. I have stood weak. Yet, there, God has met me with those same eyes He showed Peter that day in the courtyard and reassured me, "In your weakness, My power is perfect. You love Me, right? Then don't fuss about this failure, but get on with the mission that I created you for."

SELF-ASSESSMENT

On a scale of 1 to 5, how developed are you in the competency of suffering and weakness?

1	2	3	4	5
"I admit I am clueless in this competency."	"I know enough to know what I don't know."	"I can get by."	"I have a healthy skill set in this competency."	"I'm killing it in this area."

PART I DISCUSSION QUESTIONS

1. On a scale of one to five (five being mastery), how developed are you in the core competency of soul care?

2. Of the sub-competencies (spiritual disciplines, worship, doctrine, suffering and weakness), which is your strongest? Which is your weakest?

3. What is one way you can lean into your strongest sub-competencies?

4. What is a practice you can implement this week to grow in your weakest sub-competencies?

5. Who could come alongside you to compensate for your areas of weakness?

PART II

Live Relationally (Horizontal Foundations)

CHAPTER 5

PERSONAL LIFE

"The expectations are incredible." "I see my family less than ever." "My spouse is always stressed out." These are the kinds of things I hear from ministry leaders all the time, especially those in seasons of church growth. Each one underscores an inescapable truth of pastoral life: the pressure is high.

No matter the size of the church, people have high expectations of the pastor—inappropriately high. Part of this is born from the lie that because people tithe their hard-earned money to pay the pastor's salary, he is bound to them. The average pastor commonly feels the need to answer to dozens if not hundreds of bosses. Therefore, their efforts at self-care are often impeded by self-guilt: "I'm taking God's time to care for myself, when my congregation expects me to be available almost 24/7."

When ministry leaders actually do things that keep us healthy, the church doesn't always get it. If someone asks, "Where's the pastor?" answers like "He's praying" get approving nods. But if it's "He's working out at the gym. He has been there for an hour," we're bound to get some questions.

The same is true with this one: "Where's the pastor?"

"He's on vacation."

"Wasn't he just on a vacation with his wife a couple months ago?"

"Yes. That was a three-day getaway; this is a two-week vacation with his family."

Distaste and disapproval become palpable. Though the cost of our absence is tangible, the cost of burnout is much, much worse.

The Leading Cause of Burnout

The majority of what causes burnout in leaders is not the lack of spiritual engagement but of emotional, physical, and mental self-care. In turn, this breaks down your intimacy with God. If you fail to care for these three aspects of holistic health with daily, monthly, and annual habits without compromise, you won't make it. At best, you will be exhausted and inefficient; at worst, you will fall into devastating moral failure.

The exhausted life is not the more spiritual life. The leader working the longest hours is not closer to God. Some of the most spiritual conversations we can have are how to eat healthy, exercise, vacation, sleep, rest, and undo stress. The way you treat these basic needs directly determines how well you will cultivate intimacy with God, how much energy you will have for ministry, and how long you can sustain the life of ministry. We need to take our personal health as seriously as we do our spiritual disciplines.

Science backs this idea. Science reveals that the impact of stress is devastating, especially when it comes to sleep, exercise, and eating. When we sleep less—usually to try to do more—we actually do less. When we don't exercise, our mental capacity, focus, energy level, metabolism, and more suffer. And when we stress-eat junk food, we flood our bodies with toxins and stimulants, which severely hampers our bodies and brains.

So why aren't we living in these truths? Can you imagine the uproar if a pastor informed his congregation that he would not be praying or practicing spiritual disciplines any longer because, well, he just doesn't have the time to squeeze everything in? He better dust off his résumé, because he would likely be looking for work! And yet, the Bible teaches us that the body is very important. Our bodies are temples of the Holy Spirit. Health is not just about us and our longevity, but about God and His presence. If we are to serve Him well, we must learn to manage stress, take vacations, give our best to our families, and eat, sleep, and exercise well.

Manage stress

When you are under stress, you don't always feel the symptoms physically. That doesn't mean the stress isn't taking a toll on your body, your emotions, and your spiritual life. To be healthy, you've got to figure out how to manage stress in your life, and you must do it consistently.

The first solution is straightforward: get a physical every year. The doctor will check your vitals and see how your body is holding up to the pressures of your life and work. It will force you to be aware of warning signs—or stop signs—so you can take action to fix the problems.

The second solution is also simple: relax. What makes you sigh with contentment? Do that thing. The answer is different for each of us. For example, massages don't relax me, but for some they are pure bliss. My thing? An action movie. Perhaps for you it's fishing, walking, or some sort of high-adrenaline activity. The point is, figure out what makes you relax and do it regularly.

A third solution is creating clear parameters around when we will and will not work, both on a daily basis and over the course of weeks and months. Set those patterns in your life and then protect them at all costs. Perhaps you decide that you will not do ministry after 6:00 p.m. five nights a week. This means no answering calls, working on messages, or checking emails. Stick to that as best you can. Guard it. If Saturday is your day off, take it. Refresh and spend time with your family and friends. Enjoy those times and be present.

Take vacations

Another way to manage stress and maintain holistic health is to take prolonged breaks. To sustain yourself for ministry, you have to rest your brain. If you don't stop your brain from constant firing, how will you ever recharge your system? I recommend four weeks minimum of vacation time per year, and three weeks should be consecutive. Other jobs or roles may not need that much time off, but when your work is as emotionally stressful as ministry is, you need physical, mental, and emotional renewal to compensate.

Here are a few vacation tips I've learned over the years.

1. Learn to take whatever block you need to actually have a vacation. If I need a week of holistic relaxation, I really need to take two weeks off. In ministry, there is a decompression stage when you leave a space and a compression stage to reenter that space. Our work is not the kind we can easily leave at the office. For me, I need about three days to detach and another three to prepare to reenter. You might need more. Take it. Encourage your leaders to read Jimmy's book *Pastors Are People Too* to learn how to most effectively care for and champion spiritual leaders.

2. Perhaps consecutive weeks away is unrealistic for you. If that's the case, use three days at work to start

decompressing instead of using your actual vacation. Just stop thinking about work, and start dreaming about vacation. Ignore texts. I do this intentionally on work time. Some may accuse me of "stealing" from work, but you know what my other option is? Steal from my wife and kids. I figure Jesus is okay with the trade.

3. If you're married, and if you are able, take one vacation with your family, one with your spouse, and one on your own.

There will always be legitimate predictable obstacles that will threaten to steal this required time away. Take each obstacle and evaluate it. Beg, plead, and borrow from other churches if it is a human resource issue that makes your absence difficult. Every once in a while, you may need to tell your family, "We just can't do it this season." Fine. Do a longer trip next time around. But if it's becoming a pattern, then solve the problem. If you don't, you will burn out.

You may be thinking, "I just can't step away from the church for that long." That signals two things: The church is either too dependent on you, or you arrogantly think it needs you. You can be gone for three weeks straight and the church will survive. In fact, there may be a revival in your absence—perhaps the Lord reminding you that this is ultimately His work and that His name is on the line, not yours. Do whatever you have to do to make it work. But go on vacation annually.

> Some may accuse me of "stealing" from work, but you know what my other option is? Steal from my wife and kids.

Further, have your staff do the same. At Mosaic, the day you get hired, you get four weeks of vacation. You don't earn it; you can use it day one of your employment. What's more, if we find out you go a year without using it, we might fire you. That's not a joke. We tell our staff all the time, "If you aren't using your vacation, you are thwarting gospel work." You really are. You are saying you are superhuman and can sustain things other people can't, which is arrogant, shortsighted, and categorically dumb. The price we are going to pay from your burnout is far higher than the price we will pay with you being gone four weeks out of every year. Furthermore, if a member of our staff has a tragedy or even just comes to us and says, "I know I've taken my four weeks already, but I'm just tired," we tell that person take another week. Rejuvenation is gospel focused.

Give your best to your family

This prioritization of time away from work applies to vacations as well as to daily and weekly periods of rest. Carve out intentional space each week to be with your spouse, kids, and friends. Don't sacrifice your days off for ministry. Give your optimal personal days to family. I say, steal your best self from work, not from family. Always make sure that the ministry pays the bigger price. I take Friday and Saturday off because those are my best days of the week. On Monday I'm tired, so I give that to the church. We often give our families and our own soul care our most exhausted and distracted times and give our best to the ministry. If that's you, stop. It needs to be the other way around.

If you find yourself struggling to engage with your family fully on Saturday because you know you need to preach on Sunday, prepare your sermon in advance and preach it once through. It doesn't matter who you preach it to—your family, no one, a squirrel, whatever. Then write down your notes. Doing so will make you better on Sunday and get things off your mind and onto paper. If you don't think about your message on Saturday, maybe it won't be as good on Sunday—that is absolutely true. However, our primary job is not to do ministry at its very best but to do life at its very best. If being present for your wife and kids requires a lower bar of delivery on Sunday morning, then so be it. This is our calling.

> Our primary job is not to do ministry at its very best but to do life at its very best.

I've had times when I knew I didn't have my message where I wanted it to be. Often, these are the weeks when my family or kids have been particularly demanding. I tell God, "You know my week. You gave me those kids. I'm going to bring what I've got, and You do what You want. This is the best I've got with the life and the time You gave me." You know what? God has never said back to me, "Wrong move, Renaut. What I needed you to do was to be the best speaker." You know what I sense in the Spirit of God instead? "Well done. Keep your head on straight. You bring what you've got, and I'll do the rest. I know what your family needed from you this week, and I called you to them first." As Jimmy says ad nauseum, "All of life is ministry, and your family is your primary ministry."

I once heard a story about a famous professor who drove home over a bridge every evening. While on the bridge, he'd slow down and mentally set his day's baggage on the side of the road. Each morning on the way back to work, he'd slow down in the same spot and pick it back up again. He said it was his mental way to remind himself that messy ministry baggage does not belong in his house.

Discover what your tools are to leave your baggage at work and return to your family relaxed and ready to fully participate in life.

Eat, sleep, and exercise

These three disciplines are the trinity of health. Let's start with eating well. Eating well doesn't mean you turn into a health freak, but that you get intentional about what you eat. Don't reach for unhealthy, calorie-heavy fast food or junk food. When you get hungry, your stimulants have decreased, and your serotonin and dopamine levels have dropped. You feel sadness, and your brain starts searching for what last made it feel happy: sugar and caffeine.

Be wise if you eat out a lot, which most of us do, because we have many, many meetings. Did you know you can decide where you meet people? I didn't know that when I was a church planter. I used to go wherever the other person wanted to go, driving all over town and eating garbage. Now I'll tell people, "I'm in Winter Garden. How about we meet at . . ." If that doesn't work for them, then I'd say, "I'm happy to pick a day where you have the time to do that." Or I'll offer to meet halfway. It allows me to remind people that I am not God, and it lets me choose a restaurant with healthy options. Now, there are about six restaurants where I eat. I also know at least two things on that menu that are generally healthy. This affords me more time to focus on the meeting and talk with the person without the distraction of looking at the menu. Additionally, I don't eat fast food. If someone wants to meet there, I'll bring a smoothie with me, and that's appropriate.

Second, get enough sleep. Science proves that the less you sleep, the less you do. Being well-rested increases productivity and performance significantly.[8] You've simply got to sleep. Naturally, there are seasons where you just can't sleep as much as you need—for example, when you have a baby. But then how do you compensate during those seasons? You do less.

Do you have trouble sleeping? For most people, sleep issues are less about biological mechanisms and more about our habits. When we don't feed our bodies well, live in a constant state of stress, and get too little sleep, the activities we choose to help us relax often exacerbate our sleeplessness. Scrolling on our phones or watching Netflix late into the night seem like a good way to chill out and escape from the hamster wheel, but instead, they make it harder for us to rest well.[9] Instead, we should power off our devices well before bed, choose calming bedtime rituals, and try to maintain a consistent sleep schedule. If you have good sleeping habits but are still not sleeping well, consult a sleep doctor. Sleep is the cornerstone of health; it is worth your attention and effort.

Third, exercise regularly. I read an interview with a famous actor who was asked how he gets ripped. His response was simple: "My goal is to break a sweat each day." This is a doable goal. Take a brisk walk in the evening five nights a week. Get on the treadmill a couple of times. Play outside with your kids. You don't have to join a gym or push weights to break a sweat; just find something you enjoy doing that gets your heart rate up, and do it for a half hour or so. You'll add tons of energy to your body rhythm and produce endorphins that will elevate your mood and help you sleep better.

At the end of the day, remember that self-care is a deeply biblical, godly, spiritual endeavor that has deep implications in making the gospel beautiful. It creates the space and energy to engage in spiritual disciplines that produce intimacy with God. It demonstrates stewardship in the care of God's temple. It creates longevity for gospel ministry. It sets the example for our people to abandon the exhausted life and make the right things a priority, and it reminds us that we are not the force that keeps the ministry going. Self-care is deeply spiritual and extremely critical. Take the care of yourself as seriously as you attend to your spiritual disciplines. It is necessary in order to run the race set before you.

SELF-ASSESSMENT

On a scale of 1 to 5, how developed are you in the competency of personal life?

1	2	3	4	5
"I admit I am clueless in this competency."	"I know enough to know what I don't know."	"I can get by."	"I have a healthy skill set in this competency."	"I'm killing it in this area."

CHAPTER 6

INTEGRITY AND ACCOUNTABILITY

The run of Marvel movies over the last few years has brought me great joy. I have always loved the superhero narrative, and now I get to enjoy it come to life on the big screen. But my fascination with the genre is more than entertainment to me. There is a scene in a movie that forever changed how I understand our war against the enemy of our souls.

In *Thor: Ragnarok*, Heimdall, played by Idris Elba, is standing guard over the city of Asgard. His only job is to watch for any sign of the enemy, and he does it well. At a certain point in the movie, however, he appears to lose his mind. With no threat in sight, Heimdall abandons his post and begins to run at breakneck speed down the bridge into the city. Suddenly, he launches himself off the bridge and into the abyss. Just when it seems his death is inevitable, he takes out two daggers and drives them deeply into the side of a ship cloaked in invisibility. His heroic act destroys the ship, saving the city from an enemy that was trying to go undetected.

When I saw the scene, I realized that this is precisely how we need to behave toward the enemy. All day, every day, he is trying to enter the cities of our soul to wreak havoc on our lives. We are told this in 1 Peter 5:8–9:

> *Be sober-minded; be watchful. Your adversary the devil prowls around like a roaring lion, seeking someone to devour. Resist him, firm in your faith, knowing that the same kinds of suffering are being experienced by your brotherhood throughout the world.*

The devil is walking around ready to overthrow us so that we will serve his purposes instead of God's. Our missional life, our family life, our work in ministry, and the reputation of the gospel depend on our vigilance against his attacks. The problem is, like that ship in *Thor: Ragnarok*, the enemy often comes in secret, and we have been tasked with keeping watch over a lot of territory, our own hearts included. If we give even the tiniest of a foothold, the effects of the invisible will become horribly visible.

Unlike Heimdall, who singlehandedly protected Asgard from a covert invasion, we cannot hope to overcome the enemy alone. Our survival—not to mention our effectiveness and longevity in ministry—is dependent on our commitment not to be the only pair of eyes standing watch over our life and work. When we attempt to take on the enemy by ourselves, we are setting up ourselves, all that we stand for, and all that we value for catastrophic failure.

Limited Power of Accountability

Those of us in ministry are often taught, and teach others, that the primary line of defense against the temptations of the enemy is accountability. I love accountability. However, accountability is limited; it cannot be the primary force that guards the gateway to our hearts and minds.

Remember that run of church leaders I mentioned in chapter 1 who fell hard and affected the lives of many? As I reflected on their stories, I wondered, where were their accountability measures when they fell? Did they even have accountability in place? Turns out, they had great accountability. They had solid teams, great staffs, and godly elders. They followed all the standard accountability procedures, and it still failed them.

Accountability is based on behavioral control. It functions on the premise that you or I don't actually want to behave foolishly; we just know that we might if left to ourselves. Accountability does not change desire. It can only do so much in warding off bad decisions, because desire transcends accountability. Once misdirected desire is born, desire will always find a way around accountability.

This doesn't happen instantaneously. We all know that. Most everyone who sets out for vocational ministry, even those who end up committing significant moral failure, agree that personal integrity is a requirement for ministry. In fact, most intend to cultivate integrity. The downward slide happens gradually. Satan is looking for the smallest way to trip you up and send you sliding. While we should guard our hearts and minds in Christ Jesus (Phil. 4:7), we should keep watch over our toes! Leadership failure begins with a seemingly insignificant compromise.

So, should we abandon accountability? By all means, no. Accountability plays a critical role in guarding our hearts. But it isn't the only solution.

Guarding Against the
Slow Erosion of Our Souls

Accountability will not protect against our desire to lie. Something more powerful is required: intimacy. Intimacy in our relationships with God, our spouse, and our biblical community is a powerful watchman over our souls. These three relationships are the Heimdalls at the gates of our hearts. If we want to be guarded as pastors, we need to develop, protect, evaluate, and assess our intimacies.

God reveals it in Scripture this way. Solomon, the wisest man who ever lived, said, "Above all else, guard your heart, for everything you do flows from it" (Prov. 4:23 NIV). Solomon is speaking of the inner part of our humanity. From our heart is born our passions, loves, and desires. That's why we as people draw hearts in the sand when we want to express a picture of love. The emoji for love is a little red heart, not a little grey brain. Thoughts come in your head and feed your heart. From there desires grow. And out of desire grow passions. If they are the right passions, protection and wonder are born. If they are the wrong passions, sin. Your mind feeds your heart, and your heart births powerful things. You and I will give ourselves to what we love.

I'm not talking about love as a logical action of commitment, which Christians have flattened love to be. I'm talking passionate, holistic, full-feeling, full-throttle, heart's-a-pounding love—and not only the romantic kind but also the brotherly kind. That is intimacy, which is the love that compels us to lay our lives down. Built over time and regularly tended to, it is the hallmark of relationships in which you've made yourself fully known to a select few. That's the type of love we as humans pursue. When we are in love with the right things, we don't blindly pursue those things that will ultimately lead to destruction. The three primary places to pursue deep relational intimacy are with Jesus, our spouse, and a small group of friends.

Intimacy with Jesus

Are you in love with Jesus?

Ninety-nine percent of the time, when I ask people how their relationship is going with Jesus, they tell me about a sequence of things they do. To be sure, learning about Jesus is great. Understanding the life and teachings of Jesus is important. But are you in love with Him? Is your mind blown and your heart turned upside down and inside out as you reflect on the things He does in your life? Do you go through your day thinking about Him? Are you captivated by Him? Does He stir things in you? That's the love and intimacy I'm talking about.

Intimacy with our Creator is the ultimate defense from ruining your life and the lives of others. When you are in love with Jesus, you are less vulnerable. Jesus teaches this in John 14:15: "If you love me, you will keep my commandments." Our intimacy with Jesus births a love that naturally stirs a desire to follow His ways. If Jesus is not one of the stirring desires in your heart, then you will not follow Him. Jesus is not using some sort of manipulative parent approach when He says this. He's telling us that we can be at peace that the gates of our hearts are well guarded when we follow Him. If you are totally in love with God, your flesh may still be tempted to do stupid things, but avoiding them won't feel like a burden; it will be a joy. Obedience will be a response of love, not obligation. Your life will be one grand (though imperfect) expression of your love for Him, and it will look like walking in the truth.

Intimacy with your spouse

There is something that stirs in me that makes me want to be with my wife. For more than twenty years, we have been nurturing that relationship. Do I feel this way every day? No! There are days I don't want to be anywhere near the woman. Many days, she looks at me and I know what she's thinking: "I don't like you." But here's the reality: despite days that are that way, deep down inside I know I would rather die than live without Brooke. This woman, I love her. You see, while I love my wife, I am safe. I have no desire to love any other woman. I have never talked to someone who had an affair and said, "I was just so connected and in love with my wife, and then suddenly I had an affair." It's always, "My wife and I slowly grew apart these last few months or years." When you are intimate with your spouse, in love and best friends with one another, you are not going to have an affair.

It is a marker of our intimacy that my wife has the freedom to ask me hard things. She has the phone numbers to all my mentors and accountability guys and friends, so she can call them anytime she wants and tell them anything she wants. I didn't just tell them that. I told her that. "If you ever have concerns about me and the way I'm dealing with you or the kids or life and you don't call them, you are doing me no favors. Now I might be angry with you because you called them, if I'm in a really bad place. But by God's grace, you will have saved me from a really bad place." And guess what she does? She regularly touches base when she feels she needs to. Do you know how that makes me feel? It makes me feel safe.

Now, our intimacy may not protect me from momentary lapses in judgment. That's why I still have accountability measures in place, and you should, too. Let's say it's late at night, and I have to get some work done. My wife and kids have headed off to bed (which, by the way, I don't recommend should happen in any kind of regularity—the kids, yes; your wife, no). So, I'm working on my computer, and an ad pops up for cute swimsuits for my wife. I click on it. The models look good in those swimsuits. I'm tired, so I'm not paying attention to where my mind is going. Next thing I know, another ad pops up, but this one is not for swimsuits. What prevents me from clicking on that one? I would love to believe it's my integrity and deep commitment to God, but that's not always the case. Enter XXXChurch, an accountability and filtering app. I have it on my devices. If I click on that ad, it will email five of my close friends and say, "FYI, Renaut went to this website." Do I really want to explain this to five buddies tomorrow? No.

The truth is, I really don't want to look at that stuff, but I need some accountability to save me from stupid moments. My real desire is to avoid lust, but my momentary desire might betray me, and that's when accountability is helpful. There are a number of helpful filters, like XXXChurch and Covenant Eyes. Choose one and install it today.

Protection from the predator

Have you ever considered how predator animals travel in small groups, prowling for the perfect prey to attack? As a small group, they can easily work together yet only have to share their spoils with a few. Conversely, have you noticed how zebras travel in giant packs, seemingly nervous all the time, constantly alert and on watch? Zebras in particular are hilarious. Half of a massive herd will eat while the other half stays on high alert, watching for the prowling lion. Then, at some random moment, they switch. If a zebra hears, sees, or even thinks he notices a lion, he alerts the group. All will go running together to a safer area.

My friends, we are the zebras. God's enemy and ours is the prowling lion. Because we can be self-deceivers, lying to ourselves as we lie to others, we need intimate relationships with a biblical community. It helps us detect the lion before he pounces. It protects us and points us back to Jesus.

When our intimacies are intact, we have the freedom to openly and securely share our vulnerabilities, knowing that our community will become more watchful. Intimacy creates the space where people know you well enough to know your vulnerabilities and to call you out when you are lying. Because they are watchful for you and with you, they can tell when your intimacies with your Creator and family are a little off.

For example, my accountability guys talk to other people about me—not to me only. They call my wife three to four times a month to ask how I am doing. They check in with my executive assistant. How busy is Renaut? How often is he home? Does he have devotional time or just say he does? Does he take his Sabbath? I might lie, but my wife won't. My assistant won't. They'll tell them, "Renaut says he's keeping a healthy rhythm, but he's lying to us or he doesn't realize it himself."

Also, my wife and three other guys have all my passcodes. We made a deal that if we ever randomly ask if we can see each other's phones, that person has to give the phone over immediately. And if your history is erased or the password has changed you can bet there's going to be a discussion. Long, long before I make a terrible decision, I've got people watching out for me. Relational intimacy is guarding my back.

Stay Vigilant

What follows are some practical tips I take to stay vigilant against the enemy's attacks and the slow erosion of my soul. It is how I have learned to keep my intimacies intact and strong.

1. I watch.

At the end of every week I literally ask myself, "Do I love Jesus, Brooke, and my biblical community more now than I did at the beginning of the week?" Taking the time to ask and answer this question regularly is an important part of preserving the intimacies in your life and avoiding doing something stupid.

For me, the answer is not always yes. Frankly, some weeks I get to the end and find I liked Jesus way more at the beginning of the week. Some weeks, you are not going to love your spouse more—heck, you may not even like them that much. But what happens when my answer is no? It shoots up an orange flag. I now know I need to nurture the relationship. If on week two the answer is still no, that orange flag goes red and gets a skull on it. If I am either neutral or declined in my love for Jesus, my spouse, or my biblical community, something is distracting me, and I'm not keeping watch. And if that happens a third week, I'm running up the hill to do battle. We are now in a danger zone.

This kind of ongoing, frequent assessment will give you time to make course corrections before the enemy can gain a foothold.

2. I nurture.

I cultivate the intimate relationships in my life daily. Most of you know the term *disciplines of the faith*. These are biblical and historical habits that help us engage in intimate spaces with God. They are the things that put us in the soil of transformation. At Mosaic, we often call them "the works of intimacy," in part as a way of reminding ourselves that nurturing our intimacies requires work.

The question is, what works are most advantageous to the relationship in need of nurture? When it comes to God, it may be a variety of the disciplines of the faith. When it comes to your spouse, it may be date night or a small getaway. Maybe it's just being more intentional with the way we say hello and good-bye each day. This looks different for all of us, but when you're doing it well, things in you feel different and you feel in love. You are captivated by and obsessed with that reality.

3. I'm open.

Openness means I choose to be vulnerable, to live my life out of the shadows and in the light.

My first line of defense is my biblical community. These are people on my ministry staff and members of my church with whom I am very close. When I feel scared or detect the lion prowling, I ask them to watch my life more deeply. I invite them to pay attention to the little nuances in my life.

> If light is our friend, then the stage is our freedom. If the shadows are our friend, the stage is a burden.

Often, pastors and ministry leaders assume that they ought not to have friends in the church because it gets sticky. I have experienced the exact opposite. When our most intimate friendships are within our daily biblical community, we are safest from the very dangers I have laid out in this chapter. I would argue that not being open and vulnerable with people from the church they lead is part of the reason leaders can fall. If you don't have friends in your church, that's a problem.

My second line of defense are my mentors. They are outside of my daily biblical community but know me well. I say more about mentorship, as well as biblical community, in the next chapter.

Finally, if you ever listen to sermons I've preached, you'll discover that much of my journey and struggle is brought to the stage. It's my final frontier of openness. The early stages of recognizing the erosion of intimacy is the perfect opportunity to come to the congregation with vulnerability and let them know that I am with them in the struggle of dailyness. What a privilege we have as leaders that we get to bring light to darkness in front of hundreds of people. This is a freedom and a safety net, not a burden. If light is our friend, then the stage is our freedom. If the shadows are our friend, the stage is a burden.

Now, I am not suggesting you share with your congregation when you have, for example, looked up pornography. I'm talking about the stages of erosion that happen before that becomes a reality. If you are regularly assessing the quality of your intimacies, nurturing them well, and shining light into your life so that there can be no areas of shadow, you won't get to the point at which that sort of thing will happen.

Before you move on to the next chapter, it's important to assess the intimate relationships in your life. Ask yourself the following questions, and answer honestly:

- How is your relationship with God? Are you excited about Him? Do you feel intimate with Him? If the last time you were excited about God was years ago, it's time to make a change.

- How is your relationship with your spouse? Are you best friends? Do you text or call each other multiple times throughout the day? Do you want to hang around together? If things are sour and you are embarrassed to go to counseling, it's time to make a change.

- How are your church relationships? Do you see them as a bunch of people you lead because they pay your salary? Do you see them as needy or stupid complainers who just send you bad emails? Or are your best friends in that church? Are these the people you most enjoy in life? If not, it's time to make a change.

If you're reading this and the ship has already sailed—you have an addiction, you're exploring online somewhere you don't want to explore, you're taking pills you don't want to take, your marriage is secretly falling apart—don't sit in the harbor and think it's all over. It's not. Start by inviting in your biblical community. Bring light to the situation. Be brave. It's time to bring life and redemption back to your city.

SELF-ASSESSMENT

On a scale of 1 to 5, how developed are you in the competency of integrity and accountability?

1	2	3	4	5
"I admit I am clueless in this competency."	"I know enough to know what I don't know."	"I can get by."	"I have a healthy skill set in this competency."	"I'm killing it in this area."

CHAPTER 7

INTIMATE FRIENDSHIPS

Several years ago, I had the opportunity to spend a day with a ministry life coach. This man is a consultant who takes on business and ministry leaders, hangs with them for a day, and offers advice on what he sees. He's counseled great ministry leaders of the past, CEOs, and business owners. Although he gave me some truly great advice—in fact, most of what he said still impacts key directional choices I make—I disagreed with two things he said. With time, I've come to vehemently disagree with them.

One comment had to do with our adoption. We were in the early stages of our adoption, and he advised us to discontinue that endeavor, since our church was growing and reaching a tipping point where it was about to explode. His point made practical sense, but I dismissed it because my wife and I felt called to this child as if she were our own. His other comment had to do with how we vacation. Each year, Brooke and I go to my parents' beach house in North Carolina. We spend three weeks there: one with family, one with extended family, and the third week with some of our friends from church. He grimaced at the idea that we were inviting church community members into the messiness of our daily lives. He cautioned about having friendships, let alone intimate friendships, with members of our church community. He told me that our close friendships should be outside church.

His reasons for warning me against this were incredibly valid, like potential for jealousy among members, hints of favoritism, and the vulnerability of people seeing us "backstage," so to speak. Indeed, it is risky and difficult to pastor people who also see the deepest parts of your struggle. But like I said in the last chapter, the dangers of having no close friends who are also in your regular daily spaces is far more perilous. Far too many leaders manage functional friendships rather than intimate ones, or only have close friends outside of their regular orbit. These are not the friendships you need most. For me, it's been the friends in my biblical community who have saved my life.

Freedom and Support

In my life, I have a good number of close friends in the church. Proximity matters. If close, intimate friends only see you in environments that are outside your norms, they are not able to pick up the subtle hints that something isn't right. Right in the middle of where you do life is the best place to have some of your close friends.

At one point, about three years into our adoption journey, life had become really heavy. I felt the need to be present at home as much as I could. I canceled several movie nights in a row. After my third cancellation, my friends sent me a text of some guys in a van with masks kidnapping someone else. The caption said, "Next time you cancel, here's what will happen!" They saw me every week at church and could tell life was heavy and I needed my friends.

Going one level deeper, I also have intimate friendships with a number of people in our congregation and on our staff. But my friendship with two guys from my church, Flor and Scott, has become particularly close. These two men live in a similar space as I do. They've adopted kids, creating large families and the significant issues that come along with that. Like me, they both have incredibly busy and demanding jobs. They also have wives similar to my wife. I started to get together with Flor and Scott several times a month. We started texting short cries for prayer and strength on a daily basis, or just little emojis that would say, "Having a really rough day!" We meet at the same restaurant every time, eat, and then go and watch some brainless movie with hopefully as much fighting in it as possible.

Every time we walk into dinner, there is an expectation that we will share what we feel. No judgment, no advice, no questions asked—we just share what we feel. Here is the one space on the planet I can sit down and say, "Oh my goodness, I think I'm done." This is the one place I can use words and language I would be hesitant to use anywhere else. I can say anything because I know there is no judgment. It is the one place I can say things I think and feel about my wife, my kids, my life, and humans in general that would cause most others to phone a therapist. I know these two guys can graciously and confidentially handle my candid thoughts and feelings that just need a way out. We sit there and lay it all out on the table. Then we eat and we talk about random stuff.

Eventually, one of us will begin to offer thoughts about what was shared. "Knowing the truth of the gospel stinks sometimes, doesn't it?" one of us will say. It's our way of saying, "Well, as bad as we feel, we're going to need to step into the beauty of the gospel in a minute and remind ourselves of who we are and who He is so that we regroup and live in the freedom and power of what we know to be true." We preach the gospel to each other! And from there, it's a slow progression into how the gospel informs those feelings. The great comfort in that space is that I know with absolute confidence that anything I bring there will be informed by the gospel by the time I leave.

We leave our time together re-grounded in truth. Did our negative feelings go away? Maybe not right away, but we know what to do with them. We don't hide them or pretend they are not there. We deal with them and together submit them to the truth of the gospel. Those two guys do that for me on a consistent basis. I look back and try to imagine how many untruths I would have believed if it wasn't for those two friends. They give me the freedom to voice untruths in a safe place without fear of condemnation. This is why intimate friendship is a giant deal. They do not judge you, but they also push you back into a place where gospel realities inform your insanities.

It turns out God designed friendship for this purpose. Ecclesiastes 4:9–10 tells us, "Two are better than one, because they have a good reward for their toil. For if they fall, one will lift up his fellow. But woe to him who is alone when he falls and has not another to lift him up!" We've all heard this verse many times, but in my experience as a ministry leader, what I've learned is that if I don't have these close friendships in my immediate circle, then I'm not going to make it. This is a critical competency in the journey of sustaining longevity of ministry.

Foxhole Friendships

The most intimate and extraordinary friendships have been forged in the foxholes of war. It's because in a foxhole, our need for one another is not a luxury but an absolute necessity. We belong to an army of Christ-followers up against the unredeemed spaces of this life. When you face difficult things, you realize hard things about yourself you never knew existed. You need friends when you aren't yourself, leaning over you and saying, "Stay with me. Stay with me." We are in a fight together, and we need these intimate friends who are handing us weapons and having our backs as we go forward on the battlefield, just as we do for them. We are counting on them to show up with the big guns to fight beside us in our vulnerable moments. So often, at the end of my time with Scott and Flor, we'll look at one another and say, "You good, man?" "Yeah, I'm good." That's intimate friendship.

They do not judge you, but they also push you back into a place where gospel realities inform your insanities.

Foxhole friendships can also come about with couples, especially those with similar life stories. When Brooke and I stepped into our adoption story, things got very hard very fast. I tell people often that bringing my four children from Ethiopia into the family with my four biological children was very much like a collision of two tractor-trailers driving towards one other at a hundred miles an hour. The hope was that two tractor-trailers would turn into one giant tractor-trailer. The truth is that when two tractor-trailers collide, it turns into a giant ball of fire with thousands of small parts flying through the air at very fast speeds. When you've put out all the fires and gotten everything under control, you have a giant mess to try and put back together. The next decade and beyond is rebuilding a new truck with the broken parts.

During this journey, everything you know to be true of yourself is tested. You feel things, think things, and even do things you never thought possible. Everything is suddenly a struggle! Your marriage struggles, your personal life struggles, your spiritual life struggles, and everything you thought about being a dad becomes a struggle. It's a crazy ride.

By God's grace, a number of other families in our church stepped into the journey of adoption around the same time. We already had connections with them, but the trauma and intensity of the adoption experience lead us to a place of more intimate, deeply vulnerable conversations. The weight, the trauma, and the carnage that adoption brought into our homes was very similar, so it was so good to have someone to talk with who understood our struggles and would withhold judgment.

Brooke and I also—individually and as a couple—began to see our fantastic therapist, Jim Kochenburger, who also happens to be part of our community at Mosaic. Leaning in to that work with him has brought deeper intimacy to our family relationships and friendships.

Watching for Sharks

Each summer, our family vacations at the Outer Banks of North Carolina. The kids absolutely love it. They spend the entire two weeks in the water. One year, we found out that because of a strange phenomenon, the waters were infested with sharks. There had been a number of shark attacks up and down the coast exactly where we were vacationing. It seemed this year we would not be spending time in the water. Once we got there, we realized this would make for a terribly boring vacation. I spent the first three days watching the water carefully. It became clear that if the sharks came anywhere near the shallows, you could see them.

We decided to let the kids play in the shallow water. However, we had some rules. One, nobody goes in the water unless one or two adults are standing on the beach and watching very carefully for sharks. Two, when the whistle blows (and it was loud), everyone has to get out of the water fast. The adults knew that if for some reason the kids did not quickly exit the water, they had to be ready to go in the water and rescue that child.

As I watched this play out day after day, I realized this is how life works. You and I head into our day to participate in whatever God has for us. The day is full of wonder, just like the ocean, but the day is also full of dangers. There are sharks in the water in the form of temptations, traps, and all sorts of idols. For those of us in leadership, the sharks are actively pursuing us.

When there are sharks in the water you don't dare to enter the day without someone watching for the sharks. So often we leaders have no one watching our back and calling out the sharks in our waters. And even if we do, we sometimes ignore their calls and stay in the water. Leaders need watchers, and leaders need to obey those watchers. In fact, we need watchers who will rush in and drag us out kicking and screaming if they have to, because sometimes, we too are oblivious or obstinate.

Scotty Smith and Steven Smith are my watchers. Both are over a decade ahead of me in life and see what I cannot. I trust them both. They are not in my daily proximity, but they have access to those that are, including my staff, my wife, and my friends. I have told both those men that if I ever get blinded by my ministry context and start thinking too much of myself, they need to pull me out of it all. In the Old Testament, the high priest would enter the holy of holies once a year on the Day of Atonement. Legend has it (the Scriptures do not confirm this) that people would tie a rope around the high priest's ankle so that if he was not properly prepared for his task and died in the presence of God they could drag him out of the holy of holies. I'm not suggesting I'm like the high priest. I'm just saying my friends are a rope around my ankle so that they can drag me out of my foolishness if I ever forget myself. And I know they will. Who are your watchers?

Our Biggest Danger

Most leaders avoid intimate friendships. They know it's important to guard their reputation, but they wrongly think it means successfully hiding the mess. If that's the case, then close friendship in the proximity of their everyday lives is their worst nightmare and gravest danger. However, hiding one's mess to guard a reputation is just delaying and amplifying the inevitable reputation crash that's coming.

We are to guard our reputation by guarding our life. For that, we need safe places where we can work through our mess and see it healed. If guarding our reputation is guarding our life, then vulnerability and close friendships in the proximity of our daily lives are our safest strategy. Do you see why I said close friendships have saved my life and save my life each day? I want to climb out of this book and beg you to dare to develop close friendships in your church. Do it and do it now. Get some people on your beach. We desperately need gospel friends—friends who would go to any length to guard and protect.

Brennan Manning was a Catholic author who passed away in 2013. The author of *The Ragamuffin Gospel*, Manning was born Richard Francis Xavier Manning. During the Korean War, he served in the Marines, stationed behind enemy lines in North Korea. Richard's closest friend was Ray Brennan. One day while the two friends were sharing a chocolate bar, a live grenade landed in the foxhole. Ray's eyes flew first to the grenade and then to Richard. He smiled, let the candy bar fall to the ground, and launched his body on top of the weapon just in time to save his friend. Richard climbed out of the foxhole without any serious wounds, thanks to Ray's sacrifice.

After the war, Richard had his first name legally changed to Brennan.[10] From now on, his name would be in memory of the man who paid the price for him to live. At that time, Brennan took on a newfound love of life, embracing the gift of living that the Lord had placed before him.

We all need Rays in our life. Woe to the leader who resides in the foxhole alone.

SELF-ASSESSMENT

On a scale of 1 to 5, how developed are you in the competency of intimate friendships?

1	2	3	4	5
"I admit I am clueless in this competency."	"I know enough to know what I don't know."	"I can get by."	"I have a healthy skill set in this competency."	"I'm killing it in this area."

CHAPTER 8

LIKABILITY AND SENSE OF HUMOR

It's unlikely you've ever heard of a course in seminary titled "The Art of Likability and Humor." And yet, likability and a sense of humor are some of the most vital assets ministry leaders possess.

Let's be honest. Not everyone has a personality that is particularly likable. Nor does everyone have a natural sense of humor. I'm not talking about being a jokester but rather about enjoying life and light conversation, being someone who isn't severe. I love and respect several incredible people with very structured personalities. They are task-driven maniacs. While they commonly produce effective work and structured spaces of great growth and momentum, these people can be a challenge to work with and be around.

Jimmy and I have seen several cases of a church sinking in large part because their ministry leadership was unlikable and lacked a sense of humor. For most of us who lack this skill, it will not cost us the ministry, but it will cost us. We will unintentionally hurt people and obscure the love and warmth of Christ.

Your personality dramatically influences the way others experience you as a shepherd and a teacher of the gospel. Furthermore, it significantly influences the manner in which they receive the gospel that you represent. This is why you must develop these skills and shepherd people with warmth and good humor. The good news is, it's easier than you think.

How to Develop Likability

Likability can be learned. What's more, it isn't just about adding skills or behaviors; it can also mean subtracting others.

Let's start with a simple practice: smiling. Smiling is one of the essential tools of likability. Smiling endears you to others and conveys your humanity. This is a big win. It creates approachability, which opens the door for ministry.

We tend to not smile when we are focused on a task. So, as a ministry leader, when you walk around your church hallways focused on the message you are about to preach, you are going to have to get used to doing so with a smile on your face—that is, if you want likability to be felt by the people around you. Related to your smile is your general countenance and body language. Avoid scowling, stand tall, and dress presentably. These are small acts that communicate to your church, "I like you, and I care."

> Jesus came with a towel and a basin, not a green room and a private entrance.

When it comes to likability, far more important than your smiling is your service. As Jesus exemplified, likability flourishes through servant leadership. It develops as you are others-focused rather than self-focused. When I consciously smile as I walk through the lobby, that is by definition being others-focused. I am ignoring what is natural to me (focusing on the message I am about to deliver) and instead focusing on what people need to experience. That is intentional servant leadership.

Service cannot happen if we are hiding from, rather than engaging, our community on Sundays. Somehow, over the years, we have mistakenly defined the giftedness of pastors by the size of the church. The result is a fascination with the celebrity pastor. Far too many churches have green rooms, which correspond to the celebrity status of their pastor. Some pastors enter the church building through a private entrance, taking them directly into the green room. They do not worship with God's people. Rather, they come onto the stage to deliver the message and quickly exit in the same manner, having zero contact with anyone in the church. And I think Jesus weeps! Jesus came with a towel and a basin, not a green room and a private entrance.

If a pastor avoids the people of God, they are likely a narcissistic, unlikable shell of a leader. They may garner a number of laughs during the sermon, but people will always see through the hypocrisy. Their staff in particular likely know this but fear of an insecure reaction to the truth, resulting in their employment demise, keeps them silent. If you are a pastor, worship with God's people. It is important that they see you lifting your praise before the Lord. Don't hide in the green room. I understand needing rest between multiple services, but there is a difference between a place of rest and a place of escape. Be with God's people.

Doing small acts of service makes such an enormous difference. I have found one thing to be greatly significant as I've developed in pastoral leadership: I am not above doing the smallest task to help the church run smoothly. I may have just preached one of my very best sermons, but if I see that the lobby coffee creamer is out, I refill it rather than tell someone else to. Or if a kid spills water, I quickly get down on my knees and wipe it up. In my experience, these moments make a stronger impression on people than any of my sermons. They are acts of service, which build trust and likability. These are the things that make people subconsciously think, "I can be around this guy." It is an active likability. And it opens the doors to beautiful ministry.

A third aspect of likability is how we react to problems, mistakes, or crises. Take Sunday mornings for example. With all the moving parts, something will inevitably go awry. If we are locked in task mode, we are likely to respond in a way that comes across more as a reprimand. Let's say that my microphone dies just three minutes before the end of a perfect sermon because the tech guy forgot to replace the battery (there goes my perfect weekly podcast, too). What I do next makes all the difference in my likability. Inside, I may be going ballistic (and that's its own problem). Outside, I say, "Dude, don't worry about it. Nine o'clock was fine; we'll just run that one." In those moments, how we externally react is making a lasting impression that, again, opens the door to a deeper, more beautiful gospel ministry.

The Funny Thing Is . . .

Alongside likability is lightheartedness, or having a sense of humor. You will be hard to like without it. Our ability to laugh changes how people experience us. It shows them that our deepest convictions lead to joy, not severity. It reflects the way you see the world.

If you are lacking in this category, get around people and learn from them. The world is full of lighthearted, hopeful people that have learned to see light even on the darkest of nights. A great way to develop a sense of humor is to watch really good comedians who talk about regular life. Don't watch them to learn to be funny. (There are few things more awkward than someone trying to be funny by reciting the latest bit from a well-known comedian.) Watch them to learn to see what's funny in life. A sense of humor is far more about seeing life with delight than it is about being funny. I am not suggesting you become the class clown—in fact, don't. But it is important to see life from a hopeful perspective. If you lack that perspective, people will quickly discern this, because you will never laugh.

A good sense of humor requires you to be humble. Don't take yourself too seriously. The skill of allowing people to laugh at you when something happens is another aspect of likability. Like any skill, you can develop it. Every year over the past fourteen years, Mosaic has hosted some sort of annual dance event: adult prom, father-daughter dance, etc. Fourteen years ago I made the ill-advised decision to do a solo dance in the middle of the room to "Gettin' Jiggy wit It." That misguided choice turned out to be one of the best decisions I've ever made. I'm 6′ 7″, and dancing is not a skill I've developed. So when I say dance, I don't mean dance. I mean I go limp, jump around like a monkey, and do spins on the floor. It was the most awkward, weird, stupid thing anyone's ever seen. But if you talk to people at Mosaic, you'll learn that the dance is an event people look forward to every year, because at some point "Gettin' Jiggy wit It" will play, and everyone will clear the floor for the rhythm-challenged pastor.

I'll confess, at my age, it's not as easy or as fun as it was in my early thirties, but it has become the talk of the town. It makes

> A sense of humor is far more about seeing life with delight than it is about being funny.

people feel okay about the life they live and the life I live. The fact that I can be totally self-deprecating and be okay with it helps others feel okay when they get embarrassed. If Renaut can do that on the dance floor and not feel shame, they too can be okay with the lives they experience.

That is a sense of humor. It is the ability to look at a situation and put yourself out there. Be the object of people's laughter sometimes. Tell stories that are self-deprecating. Laugh at yourself. Be fun and lighthearted. It is amazing how much this increases your likability and approachability.

Likability Reflects Jesus

Likable ministry leaders preach the gospel. They represent Jesus Christ, of whom they are called to be ambassadors. Often the Gospels say that crowds eagerly sought Jesus. We know that they were certainly drawn by His authoritative teaching, the power of His supernatural acts, and their hope in the possibility that He was the Messiah. But it's obvious they thoroughly loved being around Him because of His warmth, kindness, and compassion. He was likable.

People don't want to be around people just because they have great content. Powerful words will cause some to stick around for a short time, but eventually that fades.

When we are likable, we reflect Jesus. We carry the gospel. Conversely, when we convince ourselves that we must be ungraciously hard, lest we lose our authority, we lose sight of the gospel. It's not our job to keep members happy so they will stay and keep tithing. Our calling is to lead and disciple our people into a Christ-centered, gospel-captivated space. The gospel is not supposed to feel hard. Once it robs us of our idols, the gospel actually becomes freeing and beautiful. We do not communicate that by always being the firm, strong, no-nonsense boss—although sometimes we do need to be this way. More often, we lead people well by being likable and lighthearted so that we are found to be approachable. We do that so people can relate, laugh, and connect with us. The results will be more than we could dream. We'll have all the relational equity in the world to correct and challenge our people and make healthy demands when the time is right.

If people like you, they are going to give you a ton of grace when you mess up. If they don't like you and you blow it, grace will be in short supply. You need that equity, because we are all going to make a boatload of blunders along the way.

If you want to lead your church well, then connect deeply with them and lead them out of that connection. Develop your skills of likability and a sense of humor. And besides, you'll have a ton more fun along the journey.

SELF-ASSESSMENT

On a scale of 1 to 5, how developed are you in the competency of likability and a sense of humor?

1	2	3	4	5
"I admit I am clueless in this competency."	"I know enough to know what I don't know."	"I can get by."	"I have a healthy skill set in this competency."	"I'm killing it in this area."

PART II DISCUSSION QUESTIONS

1. On a scale of one to five (five being mastery), how developed are you in the core competency of living relationally?

2. Of the sub-competencies (personal life, integrity and accountability, intimate friendships, likeability, and a sense of humor), which is your strongest? Which is your weakest?

3. What is one way you can lean into your strongest sub-competencies?

4. What is a practice you can implement this week to grow in your weakest sub-competencies?

5. Who could come alongside you to compensate for your areas of weakness?

PART III

Build the Body
of Believers

CHAPTER 9

VISION, MISSION, AND MINISTRY PHILOSOPHY

What is your most intimate earthly connection? It is not your spouse but something even closer: your own body.

Think about it. Your body is the very means by which you exist on this planet. If you lose your body, you vanish.

Your body, regardless of its shape and size, is extremely important to you. When somebody violates your body, it is a criminal act. When someone comes at you to punch you, kick you, or harm you in any way, you defend yourself. When they come at you with a weapon, you defend yourself vehemently.

Now, what is the only thing that you would be willing to lay down your body for, no hesitation? What is so precious to you that personal sacrifice would not be debated? It's not your house, your money, your car, or any other possession. It's your loved ones. I wouldn't ordinarily walk across a balance beam stationed fifty feet above the ground, but if it could save my child's life, I would start walking regardless of the risk. In my case, my bride and my children are my most precious objects. No sacrifice would be too great to keep them from harm.

The bride of Christ, the church, belongs only to Jesus. We are tasked with shepherding His church well, but she is not ours.

Isn't it fascinating that Jesus uses these two particular intimate metaphors—the body of Christ and the bride of Christ—to describe His relationship with the church? The body describes our collective self, even though we are made up of many parts. The bride describes the dynamic love relationship between Jesus and His church. Both metaphors, by their very nature, communicate that the body and the bride belong to Jesus Christ. They are His body, His bride. The church belongs to Jesus and is to be preserved and protected at all costs.

Imagine if I were traveling for a few weeks. I came to you as one of my friends and asked if you wouldn't mind checking in on my wife. I asked you to be available if she needed help. I told you I would return soon. Now imagine I arrived home and found out that three or four days into my trip, you proceeded to move into my house. At first you slept in the guest room. Then after two or three days, you thought it would be better to actually sleep on the floor in my bedroom near my wife, to protect her, of course. Then, after a few more days, you ended up sleeping in her bed. I find out that in the progression of "caring for my wife," you started to call her your wife and behave as though she belonged to you.

When I return, how would that go between you and me? Not well—for you.

Likewise, the church means a great deal to Jesus. The bride of Christ, the church, belongs only to Jesus. We are tasked with shepherding His church well, but she is not ours. Nonetheless, when it comes to developing the mission, vision, and philosophy for the church, we often gather a small group of creative thinkers, and we try to determine what *our* vision is for the church we shepherd. This very way of thinking is deeply flawed. While there will certainly be variances from church to church, it has never been our task to fundamentally determine the mission, vision, or philosophy of the church. That is God's job, and His alone.

Thankfully, the Lord has clearly revealed the church's vision, mission, and values in His Word. It is not our job to create them, but to apply them in our local context. You are likely familiar with the difference between vision, mission, and philosophy of ministry, but for the sake of discussion, let me briefly offer my definitions:

- Vison: who the church is becoming. It is the hope of her future, and how that hope informs what she does.

- Mission: what the church exists to do. It is what she should be doing week in, week out to fulfill her purpose.

- Philosophy: how the church does her work. It's her feel and her values and her rhythms. It's what you experience when you encounter her. It's what she feels like and behaves like. It's her DNA.

While it may seem elementary to review these categories, these are the essentials of ministry. We never graduate from them.

Vision: Storming the Very Heart of Hell

What is God's wondrous vision for the church?

On one particular occasion, Jesus takes the disciples to Caesarea Philippi, a notoriously evil city where people worshiped fertility gods. Locals continued to practice fertility rites, worshiping Pan, a Greek fertility god. A spring flowed from a nearby cave where Pan was worshiped through orgies and bestiality with goats. The source of the spring was known to the Greeks as the Gate of Hades. You can imagine how scary and unclean this place must have felt to a Jewish person. This was not the kind of place your rabbi takes you for a getaway. But that's precisely what Jesus did.

In Caesarea Philippi, Jesus asks His disciples, "Who do people say that the Son of Man is?" Several answers are given, and then Peter speaks up, "You are the Christ, the Son of the living God." Jesus replies, "Blessed are you, Simon Bar-Jonah! For flesh and blood has not revealed this to you, but my Father who is in heaven. And I tell you, you are Peter, and on this rock I will build my church, and the gates of hell shall not prevail against it" (Matt. 16:17–18). There is certainly some debate over what Jesus means by "rock," but that is not important for this chapter. What is clear and unquestioned is that Jesus said the gates of Hades would not stand against His church.

This is an amazing truth! It's an amazing vision. Gates are defensive structures. Jesus' words evoke a conquering church, an overcoming church, a prevailing church. The church that Jesus describes is a church playing offense rather than defense. The gates of Hades cannot withstand being defeated by the church. We are to be on the offense. We are called to go into the very heart of hell.

Our attitude is far too often a defensive posture, building gates and walls rather than knocking down gates. God's vision for the church is that she will not be overcome but will overcome darkness and death itself, empowered by the Holy Spirit! God's redemption will spread through the darkness like a mustard plant invading a garden or leaven working into dough. This should leave us both fearless and furious in our mission! Since we know how the story ends, how could we not gather as a local body of believers to be spurred on to go and invade dark and hard spaces?

Mission: Gathering and Going

The church has a very particular biblical mission. First, she is made to carry the redemptive reality of God into every corner of the earth in every generation. Second, she is made to grow, to be built up as her members gather together and stir one another on toward love and good deeds. Jesus said in Matthew 28:18–20 that we must go into all the world and make disciples. Hebrews 10 says to not forsake our gathering together. If we are called to both gather and go, wouldn't it make more sense to skip the gathering and just go? And yet, this is the gospel call of the church. We are to know God (gather) and make Him known (go).

To do that work well, we need resources, knowledge, and support. More than just being stirred up, we need help getting prepared. In Ephesians 4, Paul clarifies the mission and leadership structure of the local church. The church (organization) and her leadership are to facilitate the going and the gathering through equipping the church for the work of the ministry, namely through preaching. This includes but is not limited to facilitating gatherings. The church enables her members to serve both locally and globally. The church supports her members when the gospel work is overwhelming and exhausting. The church encourages growth and maturity through inspiring and equipping the people to have clarity and competency in the church's mission.

Another aspect of the church's mission is mercy and holiness. In James 1:27, God summarizes the nonnegotiable aspect of this mission. He says that if we want to know what He considers a pure expression of gospel life and work, it's simple: take care of orphans and widows in their distress, and don't buy into the ways of this world. Take this very seriously. If caring for the vulnerable and growing in holiness is not a major part of your church's work, you are missing the mark.

Philosophy of Ministry: The How

The final piece of the puzzle is philosophy, the way we do things. I often tell my kids that it's not just getting the job done that matters, but the way you do it. In Scripture, it is clear that God is far more concerned about how we do life and ministry than He is with whether or not we get the job done.

In the earliest example of the New Testament church, we see a unique community that grew daily. It was attractional because of the nature of its DNA. People seemed more concerned about each other than about themselves. They were deeply devoted to God and one another. Does your church sound at all like this?

> *And they devoted themselves to the apostles' teaching and the fellowship, to the breaking of bread and the prayers. And awe came upon every soul, and many wonders and signs were being done through the apostles. And all who believed were together and had all things in common. And they were selling their possessions and belongings and distributing the proceeds to all, as any had need. And day by day, attending the temple together and breaking bread in their homes, they received their food with glad and generous hearts, praising God and having favor with all the people. And the Lord added to their number day by day those who were being saved.* (Acts 2:42–47)

Here we see the words of Jesus come to life. Jesus said the greatest command is to love God and to love people. In fact, Jesus said the world would know we follow Him by our love for one another. We are told that if we exalt Christ, He will draw people to Himself. We are told to remember all that He has done, through worship, communion, and the study and preaching of the Word.

Jesus commands His followers to place others above themselves. Our lives should demonstrate a radical sense of call to love others, regardless of their lifestyle, race, gender, political affiliation, or sexual orientation. We value others above ourselves because everyone has been created in the image of God. When people encounter us, regardless of the context of our church, they should notice we are different. They should witness a group of people actively caring more about each other than about themselves. They should marvel at the resolve of the people to step into hard things.

At Mosaic Church, we have distilled this philosophy into certain key elements we commit as a body to live out. We often say we need to preach the gospel to ourselves first, then to each other, then to the world.

We preach the gospel to ourselves through what we call the works of intimacy, or rhythms of grace. You may remember from chapter 1 that these are otherwise known as the disciplines of the faith. These are gifts given to us through God's Word and through the long history of the church that allows us to work at intimacy with God so that we stay close to Him and abide with Him.

We gather as a corporate community to worship, practice the sacraments, and hear the preaching of the Word. We also gather and do life together in smaller groups we call missional communities. This is us reminding ourselves of redemption and abiding together in Christ. This is us preaching the gospel to one another.

This is being stirred up and spurred on toward love and good deeds.

Then, of course, we go out, finding spaces that are not redeemed in our homes, neighborhoods, city, and the world around us. We talk about how to invite others into these spaces and how to be redemptive in their stories on behalf of Christ.

When the weight of missional living is too heavy to bear, we preach the gospel to ourselves and engage in deep community. We remind each other that Jesus came and served us at the cost of surviving. We have a saying to help us imitate Him: "We will always serve at the cost of surviving and never survive at the cost of serving." We're not suicidal; we just believe that redeeming the hard places in this world is costly, as the process of redemption always is. It sure was for Jesus. We will have plenty of time to enjoy the fullness of our redemption on the other side of eternity. To know Him and make Him known more—that is our life now. So we invade the darkness together, empowered by the Holy Spirit, on behalf of Christ, for His glory and the expansion of His kingdom.

If we have clarity on the vision, mission, and philosophy God has given the church, then we will want to show the beauty of the gospel in the way people experience church. If we don't do attractional things because we are not "an attractional church," then we don't understand the call to make the gospel beautiful in all its facets. If we serve coffee and donuts, it's not to keep people, but to show people hospitality. The gospel is surprising, delightful, safe, warm, inviting, and many other things. It speaks to them in their context. The message of Jesus and the hospitality of His body is attractional.

One of the campuses of our church is located on Disney property. It is nothing like our other campuses because Disney cast members live a very different life than most normal suburban folks. When we planted that location, we had to get to know their rhythms and context. That's why the Disney campus meets at unusual times. The way they do life in smaller groups looks totally different. The way they engage in missional life in their context looks totally different. In many ways, you would never think we are the same church. Yet their mission, vision, and philosophy are the same as ours, as is the way they present the gospel. We make that reality clear. And yet, because the church is contextualized to the Disney culture, the outward appearance is distinctively unique.

On both campuses we make equally clear that to be called by Jesus is a call to forsake everything for the glory of Christ and the advancement of His kingdom. Jesus' call will invade you, convict you, assault your idols, and ask big things of you. What an adventure!

This requires balance that comes from clarity. Remember, the church is not primarily about the people. The church is about exalting Jesus and displaying the beauty of the gospel. When we lift high the name of Jesus, people will experience the wonder of the gospel, and they will soon discover the beauty and privilege it is to know, follow, and serve God. This is our calling.

SELF-ASSESSMENT

On a scale of 1 to 5, how developed are you in the competency of vision, mission, and ministry philosophy?

1	2	3	4	5
"I admit I am clueless in this competency."	"I know enough to know what I don't know."	"I can get by."	"I have a healthy skill set in this competency."	"I'm killing it in this area."

CHAPTER 10

NETWORKING AND GATHERING

The first six months after Brooke and I moved to Florida to plant a church were difficult. We felt completely disconnected. We hadn't started our gathering yet, so we wanted to find somewhere to fellowship with other believers. However, when you're in town to plant a new church, just visiting churches can be a minefield.

In every lobby on every Sunday, inevitably the question came up: "What do you do?" How do you answer that? "I'm your competition. I'm not going to serve or tithe here. I'm visiting to take what I can from you and go plant my own church." Of course, none of us would really say that out loud—nor is it how we felt—but we couldn't help but wonder if people had that thought.

Then we bumped into a local pastor from an influential church in our suburb. When we shared that we were in the area to plant a church, he stepped in and offered to help. "Anything you guys need, count us in. We are thrilled you are here and so glad to have another church in the community." Obviously, his words were tremendous encouragement to me.

Those kinds of interactions are amazing because they are not the norm. The fact that we all step back and marvel at how cool it was that he did that is quite simply sad. All too often, it feels like we are trying to establish a space where people come to our church instead of someone else's. We all know the lingo: "We want to grow the kingdom of God, not just reshuffle the sheep. We don't want to steal members from another local church. We are working to reach unbelievers that don't have a church home." And yet, when people leave our church to go to another church across town, it feels like betrayal. These feelings perpetuate this sense that we are in competition with each other. This mindset shifts us into a space of arrogance and protectiveness over our church. It propels us to live for our story rather than God's story. Ultimately, this sinks us.

> Far too many pastors are jealous of the church around the corner. To be jealous means that you have more of my idol than I do.

Far too many pastors are jealous of the church around the corner. To be jealous means that you have more of my idol than I do. At times, jealousy morphs into its evil twin, envy. To be envious means that I not only want what you have (jealousy), but I want you not to have what you have. I want to have it all, and I want you to lose it all. Do pastors really condescend to such paltry thoughts? In a word, yes.

Here's what should be true. We should recognize and remember that we are part of a much larger story than our little church's. Our way is not the only way. It is a privilege to participate with other churches to see our cities redeemed by the gospel— together—because we can never do it alone. It takes all types of churches to reach all kinds of people. We need to drop all the pettiness we carry against each other and be sure that we are not confusing preferences or convictions for matters core to gospel simplicity and eternity.

The Need for an Ecosystem

In Scripture, God describes His church as a body, each one of us holding a unique and essential role. Consider the view of the church similar to that of an ecosystem. Multiple churches, all looking different, play an equal part in God's redemptive story. If you remove any one part, the entire system suffers.

This metaphor became clear to me one afternoon while sitting on a swing bench in my backyard. In the back of my house I have giant oak trees that stand tall and wide and provide shade and beautiful leaves for me and the ground below. Then, scattered throughout the yard are bushes and shrubs. Finally, I have hundreds and hundreds of little grasses and wildflowers. There are just a few oak trees, a fair amount of bushes and shrubs, and hundreds of wild flowers and grasses. Can you imagine if there were hundreds of oaks? It would be terrible. The landscape would disappear, and nothing else would grow under all that shade. On the other hand, if there were no oaks, the sun would quickly wither the grass and flowers. The flowers are fragile, but yet in their number they are strong and beautiful. This is nature, and this is the church.

Whether it's an edgy church or a serious church, a big church or a small one, a creative church or a cerebral one, each plays a critical part in God's grand story. Some are great at connecting the unchurched, while others are great at developing those who already believe. Now of course, we should all be engaging the unchurched and equipping the churched, but some do one better than the other.

We know there are certainly churches that aren't preaching the gospel. A church preaching a false gospel is not just a different expression of the church; it is no church at all. When the truths being taught are issues of eternity, not just convictions or preferences, then those churches are not part of the ecosystem. They are like a foreign animal that is introduced to the ecosystem and eventually destroys it. As we discussed in chapter 3, all gospel churches hold the same essentials tightly in the left hand.

Those examples notwithstanding, we must remember that we are not in competition with one another. Each church may hold a slightly different theology or methodology, but ultimately that's part of what makes the whole church varied, multifaceted, and able to meet anyone and everyone where they are. Not any one church can do that. When you remove any one of us, there's a gap in the system, and that creates a problem.

So, if we are the wildflower and find ourselves thinking or assuming things about the oak tree that may or may not be true, how do we begin to remedy that? If we are the oak tree and assume reasons why the church down the road is still under two hundred attendees, how do we begin to change our perceptions and become a help to them or learn a thing or two from them? Enter networking and gathering.

Benefits of Networking and Gathering

I have found that networking and gathering with other area churches has at least four benefits. First, it protects our hearts and minds from making foolish and false assumptions about God's bride and unifies us as a citywide and even global church. Remember, Jesus calls us to unity. This is near to His heart. Jesus' last prayer before He went to the cross was for our unity as a church. We had better guard it. Networking and gathering are key for this.

The more you rub shoulders with other churches, the more your negative assumptions about other churches diminish. Before we planted Mosaic Church, I came from a large attractional/seeker background. Through that experience, I came to suspect that large, attractional churches were unhealthy. In fact, in a somewhat dysfunctional way, I really didn't want our church to grow large because that meant we'd have to be unhealthy. In our first few encounters in the journey of planting Mosaic, however, I found the churches that were most helpful, kind, and open-handed with everything they had were some of the large, attractional churches in our local community. As I got to know those pastors and those churches, many assumptions I had made through observation in other contexts were diminished. God overcame my dysfunction of wanting a small church and grew our church to become very large. We now hold the privilege of affording that same open-handedness and kindness to others. There are many other examples where I've learned a great deal from churches that differ from us in their methodology, and in each instance, I feel like we are better for knowing them.

Second, networking and gathering address a little-considered dilemma: the fact that ministry leaders, while always present at church, rarely "attend." I hear you saying, "But I'm in church more than anyone else." Yes, but as a pastor of a church, you don't really attend church. You preach, organize, and lead church. Church is your workspace. Sundays are your Superbowl. I get it. As a pastor, my church is not where I go to get out of my world. It is my vocational world. It is the world in which I need to do well, where I strive to see the fruit of my labor. It is not the same as attending church. As pastors, when we show up on Sunday, we are typically the ones encouraging, challenging, spurring on others—not receiving those things ourselves. But we need those things.

Imagine if you had any other vocation and decided never to attend church. What would you tell your non-pastor self? You'd lament how that is a terrible, terrible idea and strongly encourage yourself to change your path. You'd say that besides it being disobedient, it's extremely dangerous not to be a part of church, and your vocation and life will surely suffer. That's because a person who doesn't attend church will ultimately flounder and fail. It creates a very dangerous space. This is part of the reason you see pastors fall so hard when they're in their forties or fifties. When we don't attend church ourselves, we, too, will ultimately crash and burn.

We must find spaces where we are regularly hearing the gospel preached to us. Networking and gathering is my way as a pastor to be able to have the same sort of experience I commend to my congregants. Networking and gathering with other pastors and peer ministry leaders become ways of enjoying the biblical community I miss out on in the church I lead. It's not that my church is not my community but that there is a component I do not receive because of my position. Perhaps there is a nearby gospel-preaching church that meets at different times from your church. Once a month, make your way to the church, sneak in after the service has started, sit on the back row and worship the Lord! As a pastor, there is hardly anything more freeing than worshiping where you have zero responsibility. Send the pastor a note the following week expressing your thankfulness.

Third, visiting regularly with other ministry leaders and ministries expands our perspective. Because we are so deeply involved in our own little spaces, we tend to create ministries that are too narrow in methodology, focus, and theology. With blinders on, unable to see the periphery, we operate under the guise that the unique manner in which we run our church is the vision any healthy church should embrace. But God is fully alive in all those other churches as well. Again, it takes all types of churches to reach all kinds of people. When I network and gather with other pastors, I get the joy of seeing the beauty of what God is doing in someone else's church. It reminds me that I am a little chapter in a giant story, not a giant chapter in a little story.

Fourth, networking with other pastors instructs me. Larger churches can suffer from the arrogance of assuming they are more innovative simply because their creative teams are larger (or because they *have* a creative team). And yet, smaller churches are retaining some long-forgotten core values that the larger churches can rediscover or even discover for the first time if they are willing to gather together and learn from one another. Remember, sometimes small church pastors turn out to be the best teachers and pastor coaches. Biggest does not equal best in every area of life. Look at any list of the worst coaches in professional basketball history. Magic Johnson, Isiah Thomas, George "The Iceman" Gervin, Elgin Baylor, and Willis Reed appear on every list. They were NBA stars! NBA success does not always equate to quality NBA coaching. So, too, pastoring a large church does not automatically make you a teacher of pastors. Be willing to learn from pastors of any sized church.

Collective learning is extraordinarily powerful. When we are open to seek out advice from other ministry leaders, a beautiful space is created. It creates a deep sense of appreciation and unity for what God is showing others in our ministry ecosystem.

It cultivates creativity and gets everyone thinking of new ways to carry out our shared mission. We gain thoughtful perspectives we hadn't considered. And we get to see ways God is developing each of us. Networking and gathering is a critical competency because it keeps us in church, keeps us humble, and keeps our souls.

How to Get Started

Hopefully you are realizing that you critically need to be engaged with ministries in your city—now. Here are a couple pieces of advice for how to get started.

To start with, find a solid prayer group. Over the years, I've jumped into those little pastoral gatherings I'm sure we've all endured. A couple pastors gather up once a month to talk through things. Too often, they become more of a space of comparison, which becomes frustrating and unproductive. Everyone's throwing their flier on the table inviting each other to their events with no intention of attending anyone else's. Steer clear of these gatherings. Find the gatherings where you are together praying for the city or for each other. Be a part of a movement. Get involved with pastors operating in spaces you are all collectively praying for and ministering in.

Next, be intentional about making these connections. Put it in your calendar. I've found this to be the most effective way to network and gather in a pastoral context. Take one meeting block each week and shoot a quick email to a local ministry leader who doesn't fit into your pastoral paradigm. Start with this: "Hey we've been working in the same part of the city for some time now, and I hardly know you. I'd love to hear your story and catch the vision God has put in you for your church. Would you like to meet for coffee?" Meet and listen as they share their insights and you share yours. If it goes well, invite your new friend to continue to meet, chat, and encourage each other on occasion. It's not complicated. It's merely intentional.

Finally, help another church. I mentioned earlier how a pastor welcomed us when we arrived to plant. Now we do the same. Every single time I find out a church planter is coming to town, I initiate coffee. I tell him I'm thrilled they are in our city and offer our church's help in any way we can. I mean it, too. We've printed stuff that invites others to their church. We've bought entire sound systems for new churches. We do whatever we can to help that church get off the ground and be successful.

We've also made it a point to invite a number of these pastors in our community to come to church at Mosaic. Because we have a Sunday evening service, we offer a space for them to do their jobs in the morning and then come and be fed. We tell them that we don't want them to serve or tithe or give. We are honored to simply have them come and receive. We also don't ask them not to talk to people or connect for fear that some of our people might go to their church. In fact, we encourage that to happen. It's such a small way to serve other church leaders. For those pastors of the smaller churches who are plugging away harder than I can imagine, it's the least we can offer to provide a space with no strings attached.

If you are a larger church with alternative gathering times, this is one of the ways you can serve pastors. Become a safe place for other pastors to come and worship with their spouses and families. If you are a smaller church, grab your spouse and go to a gathering at a different church. (Just me saying this scares you to death, doesn't it? It's so foreign to how we've always thought.)

If you are not networking and gathering, you may not be

engaging in biblical community. You are also perpetuating the archaic sense of the lone church who does it better than everyone else. Make it a priority to network and gather with the ministry leaders in your city, nation, or even globally. We are one body with one mission, all on the same team. Let's start acting like one.

SELF-ASSESSMENT

On a scale of 1 to 5, how developed are you in the competency of networking and gathering?

1	2	3	4	5
"I admit I am clueless in this competency."	"I know enough to know what I don't know."	"I can get by."	"I have a healthy skill set in this competency."	"I'm killing it in this area."

CHAPTER 11

EVANGELISM

As a freshman in high school, I was challenged by my youth pastor to share my faith with my friends at school. I had one friend that I knew needed to know Jesus. I got my ducks in a row, made sure I memorized all the right verses, had the storyline put together, and went ready to share my faith. I knew it would be awkward, but that's just part of the deal.

After sharing my faith with him, he thought I was out of my mind. He pushed back with a bunch of ideas and thoughts. A few days later, he informed me that because of my choice to share my faith with him, he had decided to follow Satan. In hindsight, I realize he was simply being silly and sarcastic. However, for someone being silly, he sure did stretch it out. For months he would keep bringing it up and showing me more ways that he was actively pursuing the opposite of what I shared. I had totally blown it for God. This experience caused me to keep my mouth shut for a long time.

It turns out my fear was deeply misguided. I eventually recovered from that incident by realizing that just because one person so actively rejected Christ did not mean all would. Plus, I got better at communicating and answering questions, so I felt better prepared to share my faith.

Although these observations temporarily got me back on my feet, for a long time I viewed evangelism as an obligation and mandate that could make or break my chances at hearing those longed-for words, "Well done, good and faithful servant." I had received eternal life, and the least I could do—and what I should do, if I wanted to please God—was to share the good news with those around me. The result was that I came to view evangelism as a responsibility rather than a privilege. Even more damaging, I believed that people's eternal fate was resting on my shoulders. Although I never thought of it in these explicit terms, deep down I believed that people might be damned or saved based on my ability to communicate the gospel effectively. No wonder it felt like a burden instead of a freedom. Then one day, over breakfast with my family, I experienced a clarity that changed everything.

A Great Privilege

At my house on Saturday mornings we make homemade waffles from scratch. They are awesome! We grind the grain ourselves, harvest the eggs from our chickens, and use kefir we ferment in our own kitchen. We use a variety of chocolate chips, pour the batter into a carefully selected waffle iron, and make the waffles.

My kids, especially the younger ones, absolutely love to help. Every Friday night, several of them will ask if they can help with the waffles in the morning. I choose a few of them and say yes. In the morning they help me prepare the ingredients, mix everything together, add the chocolate chips, pour the batter into the waffle iron, and make the waffles. The result is a great breakfast, a great mess, and some great memories.

The truth is, it would be much easier if I just did it all myself.

Without exception, every Saturday morning, my kids do something in the kitchen that isn't helpful. They mix some wrong ingredients, they fight or fuss, they don't do what they're supposed to, or they get bored and head off to do something else when I really need them to finish a task.

In spite of the minor or major catastrophes that take place in the kitchen, regardless of what the kids do or don't do, one thing is absolutely true: the waffles always end up on the table for everyone to enjoy. I am responsible for the waffles, and I will get them done.

If the children participate, then they share in the joy of having produced the waffles. If they don't participate, it does not change the outcome. It only changes their contribution. And when the waffles end up on the table, I always say the same thing: "Hey everybody, why don't you thank Cole and Hope for making the waffles this morning?" I'm not lying. Cole and Hope certainly made the waffles. They participated, served, and helped produce them. However, their great freedom was that regardless of what they did—because I worked to orchestrate the breakfast—the waffles would end up on the table. Because of that freedom, they got to enjoy participating, instead of feeling the weighty responsibility of catering a meal for ten hungry people.

As I studied Scripture, I realized the dynamic between God's plan and our privilege of participating in it is not so different. God gives us the tremendous privilege of participating with Him in His redemptive story through sharing the gospel with others through our words and actions. When they come to know Christ, we rejoice that we have played a very real role in their freedom. Yet our great freedom is this: if we do not participate, or we participate badly, mixing the wrong ingredients or accidentally stepping away too long from the iron, at the end of the day God will still get the job done. He will not fail. His purpose is not for us to feel the burdensome weight of responsibility over others' salvation. He just wants to spend time with us in the kitchen.

The logical next question is this: If God is going to get it done anyways, why should we participate? For the same reasons my children do. We love to spend time together. Who wouldn't want to hang out with Dad and participate in something awesome, especially when the risk of failure is eliminated? Secondarily, they take part for the joy of producing something awesome on the table. Both of these are more than enough reason to want to get up every morning and share the gospel. And what freedom there is in knowing we can't screw it up.

It Really Is Good News

The icing on the cake—or whipped cream on the waffle—is this second moment of clarity I had around the same time: the gospel is actually great news.

Yes, we know it's great news, but it often ceases to feel like it once we have experienced salvation and the newness has worn off a bit. After a while, it's common for the gospel to become the task at hand instead of the wonder *in* hand. The very way we approach teaching people about evangelism is evidence enough. In seminary, I took three entire semesters on different ways to share the gospel, including strategies to make it easier. There are constantly seminars or books coming out to help us get better at "selling" the gospel. That's not to say that we shouldn't do our best at communicating the gospel, but often our tactics can become the focus, rather than the pure goodness of the message. When we truly delight in the gospel, our tactics become an afterthought. We will find a way to shout our joy from the rooftops.

When the gospel is great news to you and me, we will find ourselves weaving it into everything we say and do, not because it's our obligation but because it's our obsession. When this happens, it also changes the way people hear it. It feels less like something sold and more like something shared from good will and love.

If we think of it this way, evangelism begins with preaching the gospel to myself. I find as many ways as possible to remember the incredible mercy and grace of God I have received. I remind myself of my great need for that grace and mercy. I remind myself of the implications of that mercy and grace. I remember how free I really am that my sins are not counted against me, that my soul is rescued and made alive, that my future is redeemed and full of life, and that my purpose is restored, which means I no longer unknowingly chase after useless, temporal endeavors that lead nowhere. I remind myself of God's kindness toward me when I did not earn it or deserve it.

Active Kindness, Active Listening, Active Love

When we see the gospel as something we pay forward, so to speak—sharing the good news we have received—it makes sense that evangelism looks like modeling God's active kindness, listening, and love.

Kindness is our natural first response to the good news. It is not an agenda or the means to an end. (Neither is it *the* end. Our kindness is not enough to help anyone understand the reality of the gospel, but it helps them begin to experience it.) We are kind because God is kind. We take our example from Jesus.

Consider how many times Jesus was simply kind to someone—the lepers, the blind, the marginalized, the tax collectors, the grieving, the disciples, and on and on the list goes. Jesus did not always give an explanation of the gospel. He simply changed life after life with beautiful, active kindness. It wasn't a means to an end to bring people to redemption. Kindness was a natural by-product of redemption and rescue, and it is often our first foot forward in sharing our faith.

Our next skill is to be an active listener and observer. One year, as we were celebrating one of my daughter's birthdays, I did something I rarely do. Instead of capturing pictures at every angle to document this occasion, I put my phone down and simply experienced her celebration. All at once I could hear the rhythms of her life. It was as though I could see her life's stories all at once and experience them at the same time. I knew at that moment that I saw and knew my little girl fully, and it was transformative.

Jesus walked into the world with this level of awareness, and so should we. In the middle of a bustling crowd, He sees Zacchaeus in a tree. He hears the widow over the clamor of many voices. He feels the woman touch the hem of His coat. He sits with little children. It's as though He listened to the rhythm of people's hearts.

Jesus is the full representation of the character of God. In the Old Testament, we see it gradually unfolding. Over and over again we read that He heard the cries of His people. As you may know, the Hebrew word we translate as "to hear" means something far more expansive and beautiful. The word *shama`* means to "perceive," to "discern," and "to understand."[11] In essence, when God tells Moses, "I have heard the cries of my people," what He really says was, "I have seen and understood them." What an extraordinary thing to hear from our Creator. Even in the horror of our mess, God tells us, "I see you. I understand you. I will pursue you. I will rescue you."

This is the God we serve. As ambassadors for His character

and kingdom, we should actively listen, because God does just that. As Jesus heard us, let us hear others. (For a full discussion of active listening, see chapter 19.)

Finally, and most importantly, evangelism involves active love. God has modeled what it means to journey alongside those in need. He does not just hear us; He engages with us. Even though humanity blew it, and though we deserve death and destruction, God steps into our world and says, "I will not let you go. I will not leave you." He promises to bring redemption to humanity. Time and time again, as we get ourselves into one mess after another, God promises to be with us, care for us, and rescue us. He continues to make His presence known to us through His incredible protective love. This divinity actually steps into this world and becomes one of us.

Divinity becoming humanity is incomprehensible. Jesus, the Lord of the universe, became vulnerable, willingly taking on our weakness. From day one, He entered the world in the ordinary, in humility, in nothingness, in servitude. God who came to be with us showed Himself to be for us. He chose to feel what we feel and experience what we experience. Though He is far better than us, He experienced life in much the same way we experience life, yet without sin.

He doesn't stop there. He stays with us and somehow steps into our world and leads us. We fix our eyes on the temporal things that we hope will bring us significance, value, and peace. He sits next to us and says, "How's that going for you?" He presents questions for us that draw us out of our temporal vision and create a vision for bigger things. He leads us into new life.

God wonders with us, travels with us, and leads us into greater, deeper things. We are also called to step into other people's definitions. Invite others to travel, dream, and pose bigger questions with you. Let them know that when they find themselves in the valley, you will be there right beside them, just as Christ is with us. Engage and be vulnerable. It's about feeling what they feel and seeing what they see. Wonder with them.

SELF-ASSESSMENT

On a scale of 1 to 5, how developed are you in the competency of evangelism?

1	2	3	4	5
"I admit I am clueless in this competency."	"I know enough to know what I don't know."	"I can get by."	"I have a healthy skill set in this competency."	"I'm killing it in this area."

CHAPTER 12

GOSPEL-CENTERED COMMUNICATION

In 2007, I was praying and thinking through what was next in Mosaic's preaching journey, and I sensed God prompting me to travel through the Bible from Genesis to Revelation. At first, I assumed that God was directing me to teach Old and New Testament surveys, basically. I also knew that the innovative leaders on the national church stage were saying that to stay relevant and hold people's attention, we needed to do a new series every six to eight weeks, and make sure you change the graphic.

I tried to figure out how to get through the whole Bible in eight weeks but quickly discovered that was not possible. I then thought we could do it in sixteen weeks. It seemed more doable, but the next challenge was figuring out how to divide the weeks into neat topics and titles that would connect with the people in our congregation.

Every now and then, God makes His plans for me pretty clear and direct, and here's what He wanted me to know in the middle of this season: "Just start at Genesis 1:1 and travel chronologically through the journey. My Word will make the stopping point each week clear."

At the writing of this book, it's been over a decade. We've made it through the Old Testament and the Gospels. We have dealt with many of the letters as we encountered their chronological position in the story, and we are currently in Ephesians. In my best estimation, we will get to Revelation somewhere between 2024 and 2026.

This series has lasted a tad longer than sixteen weeks. It has also changed my life and the way I enter Scripture, prepare a message, and deliver it. It has forced a deep exploration of the gospel and how to discover it in every word, verse, passage, story, and book of the Bible—and that has revolutionized the way I preach and teach.

The Bible Is More than a Reference Guide

So many of us approach our sermons with the belief that the more relevant our topic and simple and accessible our application, the greater the likelihood that life change will take place in our listeners. But this is a slippery slope that can take us and our listeners far from the gospel.

I am especially aware of this when I am assessing soon-to-be church planters. I have the wonderful privilege of being part of a team of assessors that determines a new church planter's readiness. As part of the process, the church planter submits a recorded sermon. On some occasions, we ask that a live message be delivered.

More often than not, I hear what I call the Christian TED Talk. Their message is new, relevant, and accessible, and they use a Bible verse or two to drive their point home, but that's it. When they are done, I usually sit there and think, "I really don't know where on earth Jesus or His redemptive story fit into that talk. It would have made a decent TED Talk, but Jesus was not preached."

When evaluating any sermon, the number one benchmark is simply this: Could that same message go over well in a Jewish tabernacle? Could the message be well received in a mosque? Or a Rotary Club meeting? If the answer is yes, then Jesus wasn't preached. Far too many sermons speak truth, but they don't preach Jesus. I have heard sermons on leadership principles from Nehemiah, messages on delegation from Exodus 18, talks on parenting from Malachi 4:6, and sermons on time management from Titus 1:3. And yet, if Jesus wasn't preached, it wasn't gospel preaching. I have heard countless brilliantly delivered, truthful sermons—which were ultimately terrible because they lacked a presentation of the gospel of Jesus Christ. Whenever you preach, preach Jesus!

> When they are done, I usually sit there and think, "I really don't know where on earth Jesus or His redemptive story fit into that talk. It would have made a decent TED Talk, but Jesus was not preached."

Whatever our teaching style, the point of our preaching is not to use God's Word as a reference book to demonstrate His ideas as spiritually valid. The Word of God is not an organized anthology of cool verses to spiritualize some topic we have chosen. It's also not a book from which we try to extract obscure meaning to wow the people with our insight. Nothing frustrates me more than when a pastor inserts their personal interpretation, having nothing to do with the text, into a biblical narrative. Then some person listening says, "Isn't my pastor brilliant? He said Zacchaeus's height challenge is like our challenge to see Jesus, and the tree is like the church, helping you see. How does he figure this stuff out?" What? How dare we trivialize God's Word to become a playground for our own ideas. When we are done preaching, people should walk away speechless over what they discovered about God and His story for us, not how cool the metaphorical meaning is that we've "discovered" in the verse or passage.

I'm not anti-topical. It is easy in topical preaching to forget the person of Jesus because you are focused on the principles of Jesus! Many well-intentioned pastors unintentionally leave Jesus out of His own principles. The Bible does not tell us to exalt the principles of Jesus to draw people to Him. It says that He will exalt Himself! If you are preaching about the principles of Jesus, it must lead to His exaltation.

Each encounter with Scripture is an encounter with God through the story or context of the passage, and as such, God should receive all the glory. Our job as preachers is to walk listeners into Scripture and show them God and His great love. As we magnify Jesus and His redemptive work, people's love for Him and actions in life became more radical and Christ-like. We become fascinated with who Jesus is, what He has done, what He is doing, and what that means for us. This is gospel-centered communication.

The Challenge of Preaching the Gospel

I'm not suggesting that this is particularly easy. The pastor's challenge is significant. We are responsible to communicate the most important ideas mankind will ever wrestle with without changing them into our version of what they mean, all while speaking to a crowd with multiple, unique filters and competing ideas. Most people aren't even consciously aware of the core beliefs they hold, and yet our job as pastors is to influence and inspire thought by connecting people to God and His redemptive story so deeply that it shapes those subconscious core beliefs. To pull this off well, we must be prepared to preach a passage faithfully and accurately and in a compelling manner. That's a massive task. Thankfully, there are some strategies you can employ to be effective.

I begin by traveling into the story. Every passage of Scripture is either a story or is set in a story. What I mean is that there are circumstances that surround the author of that passage of Scripture and the recipients of that passage. We call this the biblical, historical, and geographical contexts. My professor of biblical interpretation in seminary started every class with, "Ladies and gentlemen, what are the first three rules of interpreting the Bible accurately?" We would answer, "Rule one, context. Rule two, context. Rule three, context." Context is a giant part of accurately understanding Scripture.

Once I have immersed myself in the story of the passage or the story that surrounds it, I begin mining for the idea. There is a huge difference between creating an idea—making up a meaning—and discovering one. I like to ask, "What does the story tell us about God? About His love and mercy? About how He changes our lives? About how we respond?" Remember, God is always multitasking. In every passage, there is more than one idea. That's part of why you can come back to a passage two years later and see something you hadn't seen before. It's not because you can create another metaphorical concept that does not really exist but that God has layered so much in every verse and passage. I have found that even though you may find more than one idea, focusing on one idea is helpful to this generation. Choosing the right idea for that day must be a work of the Spirit.

Next, we test the idea we think we discovered. This simple process reveals if the idea we extracted is accurate. First, we check and see if this idea fits the greater biblical context. Does any other part of Scripture confirm it? If yes, we can trust it. If no, we need to ask, does any part violate it, either directly or indirectly? If the answer is yes, that's not the idea we are looking for.

Once the idea is tested, we need to simplify it as much as possible. The key is to remove the complexities and questions that may be layered into the idea. It's not that you won't deal with the complexities and questions in the sermon. It's just that we must start with the most basic part of the truth we found and build from there. This will also help us keep the main idea the focus in our delivery.

Let's use the story of Zacchaeus's encounter with Jesus as an example. Luke 19 tells us that Jesus was going through Jericho on the way to Jerusalem. As He passes a crowd, He sees Zacchaeus perched in a tree. Jesus stops walking, looks right at Zacchaeus, and yells emphatically, "Zacchaeus, hurry down from that tree because I need to stay at your house tonight" (Luke 19:5, VOICE). Now, Jesus didn't randomly, suddenly figure out Zacchaeus's name. Unbeknownst to anyone else, Jesus had already planned to stay at Zacchaeus's house that night. He was well on His way before the chief tax collector had any idea that Jesus knew his name.

In order to drill down to the main idea of the passage, we have to ask ourselves how it happened that Zacchaeus ended up in that tree in time for Jesus to pass by. There's only one answer: God is sovereign in Zacchaeus's story. And a God that is sovereign in his story can be trusted with my story. When you preach this passage, you may talk about the other layered truths: God's pursuit of us is intentional and purposeful; He knows our name; when He rescues us, it will change everything, all the way to our deepest ideas and longings. These are all part of what we will deliver to people. But the main idea is the incredible, mind-blowing sovereignty of God.

Our last step goes into the larger story of Scripture. We must link the main idea to the *big* idea. What is the big idea? It's the same for every sermon: the redemptive story of God, the gospel. Every truth you will discover in Scripture is in some beautiful way connected to the gospel. Every passage either reveals, expands, clarifies, or gives implications of the gospel. So in your sermon, always take it back to the gospel. What does the text say about our rescue (His grace and mercy), our restoration and mission (our new identity in Christ), or our redemption (our future hope)? How does this idea illuminate the redemptive reality of Jesus? Once you have clarity, you are ready to prepare to transfer this idea or truth you have discovered to the people you are called to shepherd.

Be the Tour Guide

In 2011, my wife and I had the opportunity to visit Rome for a few days. While planning the trip, my wife came across a guided walking tour through the city. Our private tour guide would customize the day around a particular historical era. It had a pretty high price tag. Honestly, it was the most expensive thing we did in Rome, and it cost us some other things we could have done. We risked it and spent the money. It was the very best money we have ever spent on any trip we've ever been on.

This man had spent over twenty years studying the city of Rome and the crazy details you and I would never have learned in school. He was passionate about the city and painted the wonder and beauty of Italy's capital in ways we could never have imagined. Often, he would say, "Do you see that wall and how it's two different shades?" or, "Do you see that street and the way it curves?" or, "Do you hear the way the sound travels from that central court all the way here?" He would then proceed to open our eyes to the hidden wonder in all those settings, and it all came to life. It was as though we were transported back in time to a new world and could see, smell, taste, and hear it. It was an amazing day.

Every weekend, we have the privilege of being the tour guide for the church we shepherd. We have the honor of walking people into the wonder of the story transpiring in God's Word and bringing it to life. "Do you hear that conversation between Jesus and that person?" "Can you see the struggle in that person's eyes?" "Can you feel the tension in the crowd?" We then proceed to unpack the wonder of the unseen, which we have spent hours, days, months, and even years discovering.

So how do we do this? We start by setting the scene, transporting people into the story. This is best accomplished through the historical context of our sermon text. We convey this by bringing the events and people surrounding the passage to life. Once the scene is set, find the best time to introduce the idea that God led you to in the story. This is the part where you say, "Do you notice what's happening right here? Did you hear what he or she said? Did you see how God responded to that?" You direct the focus of those you are leading through the story to notice particular details that will set up their discovery of the main idea. Once the idea is discovered or revealed, we begin the process of planting this idea deep within the hearts and minds of the congregation.

Help Them Discover Truth Themselves

To plant an idea into someone's heart—remember, God is in charge of the growth—we must connect them to the idea on an emotional level. Humans connect far more to things we feel than to things we simply think. This means moving the idea into the deeper parts of the human soul. I have found several strategies helpful here.

One is to hint rather than state something outright. A truth always sticks better when someone "discovers" it themselves, rather than simply being told. I often say things like, "Did you catch that?" instead of "What just happened is . . ." This seems silly, but it's the difference between an idea planting and idea passing through. The movie *Inception* hangs on this idea. The main characters are hired to change someone's mind and actions. They don't do it by putting together the world's best lesson or lecture. Instead, they infiltrate the man's subconscious and adjust his dreams so that he arrives at the desired decision on his own. It's a brilliant illustration of the power of engaging a person's thought life.

> Telling good stories and getting people to laugh isn't about delivering a better speech or having people like your sermon more.

Story and humor are also fantastic ways to move from intellectual connection to emotional connection. Telling good stories and getting people to laugh isn't about delivering a better speech or having people like your sermon more. It is a critical skill in helping truth connect deeply with people's souls.

It is also helpful to remember that your passion and excitement for the wonder of what God has shown you is contagious.

We all get more excited about something when someone else is excited about it. And frankly, if you are not blown away by what you have found, then you are not ready to preach it to others.

After we have emotionally connected people to the truth of the passage, we help them envision it in their very real, everyday life. To do that most effectively, get naked. Obviously, I'm not suggesting you start tearing your shirt off on stage. I am suggesting that you bring your life to the table. I think we as pastors have often thought our job is to present a picture of what it looks like to be mature and complete, not lacking anything. Yet this is not our true experience. Rather, what people really connect to is seeing us discover how God's Word really does speak to my crazy, unpredictable, messy life. I'm struggling like they are, and God is refining me too. I often say, "All I bring to the table is the gospel and my life." I show people the beauty of God and His redemptive story and how that collides with and shapes my day.

Finally, I raise the question: What if this idea we just discovered is actually true? What if we believed it? How would that change our day, our week, our life? "Here's how it's already shaping mine. How about you?" Again, I don't tell people how it should shape their life. I only offer my life and let them discover it for themselves. Often, the way it shapes me is a great starting point for others, but I let them wrestle with the truth themselves.

Our job is not behavior modification but gospel proclamation—delivering the wonders of God to produce transformation through God's working. The goal of our preaching is not simply to help people understand the Word of God but to help them hear His voice. I get to be the portal for others to enter God's Word and see what He has for them. I want to help people see Jesus in the Scriptures.

If we enter the Scriptures looking for some principle to give the people that will help them live better lives or behave more appropriately, then we will likely preach message after message missing Jesus. However, if we enter the Scriptures looking to learn about God's redemption, then we will preach Jesus and Him exalted—and our awe will increase! In everything we explore, we should seek to see what makes God more awesome, what makes the gospel more beautiful, what makes our freedom more visible. Every passage, every book—the whole Bible is a display of God's wonder and an invitation to respond to His love.

So what does it all boil down to? It's not about your communication strategy as much as it is your own clarity about the gospel and its central place not only in Scripture but in your life. Make Jesus bigger. Invite people to trust and follow Him in every detail. Exalt Christ, and He will draw people to Himself.

SELF-ASSESSMENT

On a scale of 1 to 5, how developed are you in the competency of gospel-centered communication?

1	2	3	4	5
"I admit I am clueless in this competency."	"I know enough to know what I don't know."	"I can get by."	"I have a healthy skill set in this competency."	"I'm killing it in this area."

PART III DISCUSSION QUESTIONS

1. On a scale of one to five (five being mastery), how developed are you in the core competency of building the body of believers?

2. Of the sub-competencies (vision, mission, and ministry philosophy; networking and gathering; evangelism; gospel-centered communication), which is your strongest? Which is your weakest?

3. What is one way you can lean into your strongest sub-competencies?

4. What is a practice you can implement this week to grow in your weakest sub-competencies?

5. Who could come alongside you to compensate for your areas of weakness?

PART IV

Lead the Body of Believers

CHAPTER 13

LEADERSHIP

One city, two leadership conferences, and a dozen well-known leaders. One group of leaders allowed me to witness the practice of Jesus-centered leadership, while the other made me sick to my stomach.

On one side of the city, the conference had just concluded. As the participants filed out, the speakers met backstage in the green room. Several snacks had been provided for the speakers, all well-known "celebrity" spiritual leaders. As they talked, one speaker playfully threw a handful of crackers at another across the room. That was all it took to launch a food fight that resulted in a trashed green room that more closely resembled an unsupervised middle school cafeteria. When the conference director, who had spent months working behind the scenes to prepare for this mammoth event, began to clean up the mess, one of the speakers told him not to touch anything. They were paying for the hotel and they had a right to trash the room. Hotel employees would come in later to clean up the mess. And with that statement, the leader of the conference dumped the bowl of remaining crumbs on the floor. The conference director, a personal friend, quit later that night. The stench of inflated, narcissistic leadership was more than he could bear.

Meanwhile, across town, another conference on leadership was winding down. Two full days of excellent teaching had everyone excited to begin practicing what he or she had gleaned. Several of us were driving away from the host church—a megachurch—when my friend Wesley realized that he had left his Bible there. We turned the car around and headed back.

When Wesley walked into the large hall that sixty minutes prior had been packed, he heard a vacuum and assumed the church janitorial team had begun the cleanup. To Wesley's surprise, vacuuming the floor was the lead pastor of the host church. Only an hour earlier, this pastor had concluded the conference by delivering a powerful message on leadership. He was the primary speaker at the conference, and his messages had clearly made the greatest impact. Wesley stood for a moment in the darkness of the entry and watched this man work. He specifically remembered this pastor walking out of the room with the rest of the leaders, talking in the parking lot for fifteen minutes and then getting into his car and driving away. When Wesley walked into the room to pick up his Bible, he startled the pastor who was clearly a bit embarrassed to have been "caught" performing janitorial duties.

The following morning, we returned to the church for a follow-up meeting. The lead pastor/mystery janitor was out for the day. When we saw his administrative assistant, we inquired as to why this high-caliber leader was doing menial labor. His assistant responded with a few sentences I will never forget. "Please, don't tell anyone. He always asks to be assigned a couple of menial tasks around the church, which he will perform—100 percent behind the scenes—to remind him that the real power in leadership comes via service of others."

Two conferences. Two vastly different pictures of leadership.

There is a massive difference between power leadership and servant leadership. When we believe we are better than anyone else, power becomes the controlling idol in our life. Regularly reflect on how you treat hotel maids, flight attendants, and construction workers. Do you make eye contact with staff at a restaurant? What is your heart attitude if you are confronted by a TSA agent, a police officer, or an usher at a sporting event?

Sadly, we live in a day when the celebrity pastor continues to dominate the leadership landscape. Rather than evaluate a leader by his acts of service, we judge by book sales, Twitter followers, and Instagram likes. We have replaced the towel and the basin for a stage and an audience. We make massive assumptions about a person's backstage solely based on what we see on the frontstage. We have exchanged authentic godly character for perceived leadership talent. The depth of one's soul has been swallowed by the breadth of one's audience.

Leadership is commonly misunderstood. Our culture sees leadership as strength, wealth, influence, and the ability to gather an enormous band of faithful followers. In reality, anyone can lead. Christ-centered leadership begins with an assessment of the controlling idols in your heart.

I have been disheartened and discouraged when I attend leadership events that are built on the underlying assumption that leadership is a rare gift granted to only the chosen, gifted few. Leadership has absolutely nothing to do with title, legacy, or position. Some of the very best leaders have no title, position, or designated authority and have no desire to promote their work on a national stage. The man or woman pastoring a church of ninety-five can lead as effectively as a pastor of a church of ten thousand. And in some cases, the smaller church pastor may be the more effective leader.

The Idol of Power in Leadership

Power is a life-controlling, mind-altering, heart-shifting drug. Alongside approval, comfort, safety, lust, and control, power has long been known as one of the deep idols. As such, it can only be dealt with at the heart level. If idols are not confronted there, behavior will not change. Idols twist our hearts into knots. Heart idols lead us to a place where we are not just wounded by criticism; we are devastated. And the number one idol that adversely influences leadership is power.

John Calvin wrote, "The human heart is an idol factory. . . . Every one of us is, from his mother's womb, expert in inventing idols."[12] An idol is a false yet functional god. Idols function on balance, like a teeter-totter on a playground. When one side is down, the other side is always up. When we elevate anything to idol status, we conversely must demonize anything that contrasts with our obsession. If my child's performance is my idol, I intuitively demonize other children. If my favorite sports team, the Kansas Jayhawks basketball team, were an idol (remember, this is just for the sake of illustration), I would naturally demonize Kentucky, Duke, and North Carolina basketball (as if they would need any help being demonized!). If my political party is where I find my self-worth, I will bash rival political perspectives. If my reputation is my idol, I will belittle my peers. If my church is my idol, I will find significant fault with other churches.

Commenting on the idol of power, N. T. Wright has written,

One of the primary laws of human life is that you become like what you worship; what's more, you *reflect* what you worship not only back to the object itself but also outward to the world around. . . . Those who worship power define themselves in terms of it and treat other people as either collaborators, competitors, or pawns.[13]

Power used to control rather than serve is an empty idol that will not offer enduring contentment. It always leaves you wanting more. But be encouraged! Like the pastor who successfully led a large conference and then secretly stayed behind to do janitorial work, Christ-like character is achievable.

The primary purpose of power is to serve the powerless. Power is meant to bless and to lift up those around you. As a pastor, it is essential that you and those around you regularly ask hard questions regarding the power you have from the Lord:

- How are you using your power and influence to serve those within your local congregation, including single parents, the unemployed, and those who have self-isolated?

- What are you doing to serve those in your community who lack opportunity to advance their life situation? In what ways are you serving the poor and the oppressed?

- What have you done in the past week to use your power to lift up nearby churches? Have you used your influence to offer trainings or share resources?

There are countless illustrations of those in leadership who were given incredible amounts of power, used their power to serve the greater good, and then humbly surrendered their power. Perhaps my favorite comes from the life of Lucius Quinctius Cincinnatus.

In 458 BC, the armies of Rome were simultaneously fighting a war on two fronts. The Roman Senate had sent two of its best leaders to defend Rome against the advancing forces of the Sabines and the Aequi. Rome fared well against the Sabines but not the Aequi. They were quickly surrounded, with no hope of re-provision; all the Aequi had to do was starve them out. In a heroic act of bravery, five Roman riders were able to break through and make their way to Rome, where they reported their dire predicament to the Senate.

The Senate knew there was one hope: Cincinnatus, a sixty-one-year-old former leader they continued to hold in the highest esteem. An obscure provision in the Roman constitution allowed for the appointment of a dictator in times of crisis. The dictator would have absolute, unchecked power to control every aspect of the Roman republic. The Senate sent a delegation to a small farm in the rural countryside to speak with Cincinnatus, who earlier had been forced into exile.

As the delegation arrived at his humble farm, Cincinnatus abandoned his plow, approached the men, and famously shouted, "Is everything all right?" The men informed him of the grim situation and offered him the position of Roman dictator. With a heavy heart, he called to his wife, Racilia, to bring him his toga, a sign that he accepted the challenge. Cincinnatus mounted his horse and headed for Rome.

In only a couple of days after arriving, Cincinnatus mobilized the citizens of Rome, collected critical weapons, gathered the necessary provisions, recruited an army, and set out to rescue the trapped Roman forces. They took twelve times the standard allotment of spears and by nightfall had surrounded the Aequi forces. Over the coming days, they used the spears to construct a makeshift wall that trapped the Aequi army. The wall completed, Cincinnatus personally led the charge, attacked the Aequians, and, in a matter of hours, won a decisive victory.

Cincinnatus and his army returned to be welcomed as heroes who saved Roman citizens from certain slavery and possible death. As dictator, Cincinnatus had every legal right to reign as supreme commander of the entire Roman Empire. But he immediately resigned and returned to his farm to continue to plow his fields. In total, he was the supreme ruler of the Roman Empire for only sixteen days. (Amazingly, in 439 BC, a similar situation arose. But this time, Cincinnatus held the post for just twenty-one days. He then returned to his farm.)

Cincinnatus is a beautiful picture of using power for the common good of the people. He was the rare combination of integrity, leadership, civic virtue, simplicity, modesty, and humility. On two occasions he was in a position to lead the most powerful empire in the world, and on two occasions he immediately surrendered power once the task was accomplished.

In Cincinnati (named for Cincinnatus), there stands a statue of Cincinnatus. In one hand he holds the documents of government, in the other a plow. In the halls of government around the world, may his tribe increase.

Four Types of Leaders

Painting with a broad brush, there are four types of leaders: the visionary leader, the structural leader, the measurement leader, and the social leader. Understanding the unique characteristics of each leadership style will help you to more effectively operate in your particular area of gifting while enabling you to more effectively build a complementary team that encompasses all four leadership types.

The **visionary leader** paints a stirring picture of what *could* take place. He or she effectively shares about organizational transformation leading to cultural transformation that could happen if everyone rows the boat in the same direction. In the business world, the visionary leader would be most commonly defined as the CEO or president. He or she has the power to cast vision and the authority to put it into action. They inspire collective purpose in their team. The visionary leader is more of a conceptual thinker than a sequential one.

Next is the **structural leader,** who immediately begins to ask the tough but absolutely necessary questions: How can we mobilize the vision? Who—to continue the rowing metaphor—fills the boat? What partners can be counted on to be a part of the movement? The structural leader is commonly referred to as the chief operating officer. This person focuses on systems and infrastructure. This is a management leader. This is the vision integrator. This is the leader who builds what's on the blueprint. While the visionary leader paints a picture of the destination, the structural leader creates the roadmap.

The **measurement leader** sees decisions in dollars. How much will this particular initiative cost? How will the funds be raised? How will this new idea impact the current budget? The questions regarding finances go on and on. In the business world, this person might serve in the role of the chief financial officer. In most churches, this person is a volunteer, commonly serving as the chair of the finance committee.

Finally, the **social leader** wonders how projects and initiatives will impact staff relations. If we are going to partner with churches, how do we select these churches? How does our team deal with internal conflict? In the business world, this person might serve in HR or counseling.

When working with leadership teams, I regularly draw a

four-quadrant diagram that depicts the four styles of leadership. I then ask each staff member to place himself or herself somewhere on the leadership grid. People generally fall into one primary category. I allow other team members to push back if they believe a person has incorrectly self-assessed. If five of the twelve staff describe themselves as strong visionary leaders, we have a problem. If there are no sequential leaders, I am guessing that the church is long on talk and short on action. If the room is filled with conceptual, sequential, and relational leaders, I can guess that the church is regularly overextended financially.

Effective leaders build teams that incorporate and appreciate different styles of leadership. The most effective teams work to engage unusual and fresh perspectives and freely work across factions. This is the difference between technical work and adaptive work—a critically important leadership concept.[14] In technical work, the problem and solution are both immediately clear, whereas in adaptive work, both take time to emerge. Technical work requires efficiency, whereas adaptive problems demand experimentation and openness to new ideas. Technical problems can be scheduled into a defined timeline; adaptive problems operate apart from realistic interval boundaries. When facing a technical issue, the goal is to fix the problem. In adaptive work, the goal is to make progress. Adaptive plans are designed to bring life as opposed to drain life. The plan may be changed tomorrow to address problems with the plan you encountered today.

Each of the four leadership styles regularly face both technical and adaptive challenges. Clearly identifying your dominant leadership style and determining the nature of the challenge allows leaders to more effectively serve in the areas of their natural strengths.

In summary, the idol of power is to servant leadership what kryptonite is to Superman. During the early years of pastoral ministry, I wish I had understood that. I wish I had had the confidence to bring in voices that differed from mine. I wish I had understood the difference between technical leadership and adaptive leadership. I wish I had led more like Jesus.

SELF-ASSESSMENT

On a scale of 1 to 5, how developed are you in the competency of leadership?

1	2	3	4	5
"I admit I am clueless in this competency."	"I know enough to know what I don't know."	"I can get by."	"I have a healthy skill set in this competency."	"I'm killing it in this area."

CHAPTER 14

LIFE PLANNING AND MANAGEMENT

Ryan was elated when he learned that the position of lead pastor included four weeks of vacation, two weeks of study leave, all major holidays (except Easter and Christmas), and the week between Christmas and New Years, which was given to the entire staff as a year-end thank you. In total, Ryan would have close to two months to vacation with his family, prepare for sermon series, spend time working around the house, and just enjoy life. His wife, Karen, knowing Ryan's tendency to work long hours, was guarded in her optimism that this might finally be the church where they could restore a measure of balance to their family. Now entering year five in his role of lead pastor, Ryan and his family had enjoyed four weeks of vacation—in total—over five years. What began with so much promise quickly turned into a life with limited breaks, few boundaries, and little privacy.

We live in a world dominated by reactive busyness. Tragically, I have watched leaders of churches implode through a destructive cycle of work. I regularly meet with pastors struggling with issues of life planning and management. When I encourage them to create work boundaries that will protect time with their spouse and children, they often hang their head as if assigned an impossible task. And all too often, the church does not help, as busyness is equated to spirituality.

The most common call PastorServe receives revolves around the challenge of balancing family and ministry. The problem frequently sounds something like this: "I'm struggling to balance family and ministry. There is an unresolvable tension between the endless demands of my ministry and the time I know I should be spending with my family. I don't know how to resolve the strain. I feel as if I have no boundaries in my role as a pastor. When I spend an appropriate, healthy amount of time with my family, I feel guilty, like I am cheating the church."

Our response has been the same for more than two decades: "While we appreciate the tension behind the question, you are thinking of the issue in an *unbiblical paradigm*. Here is the reality you must grasp if there is indeed deep life change: all of life is ministry, and your family is your primary ministry."

Practically, what does this mean? It means that when a pastor leaves the church office to spend time at their son's football game, they are leaving their secondary ministry for their primary one. Going back to the story of Ryan and Karen, it means that if Ryan ducked out of a staff meeting thirty minutes early to attend his daughter's dance recital, he would be prioritizing his primary ministry. Once a church understands this, it will fundamentally change the way the church body treats the church staff.

Reading the Gauges of Life

It helps to understand your soul as an engine. You need fuel to run, fluids to stay healthy, and regular maintenance so you don't break down. As such, leaders must understand their gauges—signs that they are in good health. If you are a part of a leadership team, I encourage you to regularly share your life gauges with a trusted colleague. These are the gauges you should keep an eye on.

Emotional energy

This area speaks to our experience of anxiety, over-commitment, feeling excessive pressure, feeling underappreciated, and feeling trapped or restricted. All of these drain our tank. Do you feel free to connect with a counselor? Do you take one full day off every week? Have you set aside time for your next vacation? For some portion of every day, do you turn off your email and internet access to fully engage with family? Do you laugh several times each day? Do you daily listen to music? Do you find your work meaningful? Are you carrying secrets that you fear being discovered? Do you have habits which result in guilt and shame?

Physical energy

My suggestion for maintaining physical energy? Eat well (5 servings of fruits and vegetables daily), exercise five days a week, stretch daily, get a minimum of seven hours of sleep each night, drink enough water, have no more than four alcoholic beverages per week, avoid loose tobacco, and have a full physical every year. It may sound like a lot, but trust me: these disciplines will return more time and energy to you than they take.

Relational energy

Are you a part of a circle of friends who accept you for who you are? Is there a judgment-free zone in your relational life? Do you have a best friend or soul mate? A full tank would indicate that there is nothing unspoken between you and your spouse or family. Do you hug someone every day? Are you spending more time with people who fill your tank (replenishing) or drain your tank? Are you comfortable being quiet while with others? These questions can help you discern if you need to invest more in your relationships.

Spiritual life

Some questions to consider asking to get a read on this gauge are: Are your daily choices deepening your walk with the Lord? Have you set aside daily time for prayer, worship, and reflection? Do you practice the spiritual disciplines of fasting, solitude, and journaling? Do you daily notice and express thanks for the natural beauty of the world around you? Upon awakening, do you acknowledge the mercies of the Lord before you begin reviewing your to-do list? Are you regularly repenting? Are you daily growing more dependent upon Jesus? Not all of these are explicit biblical commands, but they will help you with the biblical command to love God.

Intellectual energy

Do you read for pleasure? Are you regularly engaged in learning something that has absolutely no relation to your work? Do you have intentional time to reflect on your successes and failures? This area also speaks to engaging in professional development, having a mentor or coach, and being a mentor or coach.

While all areas can run dry, relational energy is one area that tends to overwhelm those called to ministry leadership. Early in my years as a pastor, I felt tremendous pressure to spend the overwhelming majority of my time with people in need. My idea of shepherding was to reactively respond to the needy, seldom reaching out to people who filled my tank. I prioritized the care of others while allowing my own soul to wither. I was at the front of the line to give help and the back of the line to receive help. While that may sound noble, that mindset is unsustainable for any significant length of time. Unquestionably, there are seasons of tireless service. But over the course of one's life, godly rhythms are indispensable. I encourage you as a pastor to intentionally spend time with people who relationally, intellectually, and emotionally replenish you. While there must be a balance (there will always be times of reactive ministry where you are at the back of the line), it is essential that you construct the necessary boundaries to allow for replenishing relationships.

The first step towards refueling your life—and then establishing routines for health—is to conduct an honest personal assessment. All too often, our life is void of the rhythms essential to fully living before an audience of one. An assessment can begin with the following questions:

1. In what areas of your life do you need renewal, rest, focus, etc.?

2. What changes would you like to make in the rhythms and pacing of your personal life and ministry?

3. What are you presently doing in your workplace that could be effectively done by someone else?

4. In what areas of your life do you need spiritual and emotional healing? Are there life compartments that you have closed off and refuse to visit?

5. What are some healthy habits you'd like to integrate into your personal life and ministry that are currently missing?

All too often, the urgent demands of leadership crowd out the necessary work of slowing down, evaluating our lives, and making the appropriate adjustments. Self-assessment takes courage, as few enjoy looking behind the curtain to discover what lies deep within. Self-care can be particularly hard for people wired to be caregivers. Most ministry leaders do not burn out because of the demands of ministry but because of the demands of everyday life.

Coming to Terms with Limited Capacity

In *Pastors Are People Too,* I pressed the argument that everyone has limited capacity.[15] Everyone has 168 hours a week in which to work, sleep, eat, love their spouse, nourish their children, invest in personal relationships, minister to the lost, exercise, relax, and so on.

Author Marc Levy's compelling analogy comes to mind:

Imagine that you've won a contest, and your prize is that every morning a bank will open an account in your name containing eighty-six thousand four hundred dollars.... Everything you fail to spend is taken from you that night. You can't cheat, you can't switch the unspent money to another account: you can only spend it. But when you wake next morning, and every morning after that, the bank opens a new account for you, always eight-six thousand four hundred dollars, for the day....

We all have that magic bank account: it's time. A big account, filled with fleeting seconds. Every morning when we wake up, our account for the day is credited with eighty-six thousand four hundred seconds, and when we go to sleep every night, there's no carryover into the next day. What hasn't been lived during the day is lost; yesterday is vanished. Every morning the magic begins again.[16]

When pastors manage their time well, they can lead the church, love their spouse and children, spend time in personal worship and devotions, exercise five mornings a week, get a healthy amount of sleep, engage in redemptive relationships, eat, rest, and effectively do what the average week demands. And yet, the unexpected inevitably creeps into every week. Every activity drains already limited capacity. For example, in a week when there are extra board meetings, you predictably get less sleep. Or, if you catch up on sleep, it may result in you having fewer hours to work. When a marriage is in crisis, you spend additional time with your spouse, which may mean less time exercising or working. In everything we do, there is a tradeoff. We simply can't magically add hours to a week. Every choice impacts another area. We all live with limited capacity.

One of the biggest problems facing ministry leaders is the burden of the unrealistic job description. I have reviewed job descriptions in which I conservatively assigned hours to weekly standard tasks that added up to more than 125 hours. Any job description that cannot be fulfilled in fifty hours per week is doomed to result in fatigue, failure, frustration, and self-reproach. Take time to review your job description. Can you really fulfill the expectations placed on you in fifty hours a week? Evaluate an average week. How much time do you want to spend nurturing your marriage and family, your primary ministry? How much time should be spent sleeping, exercising, and resting?

At PastorServe, after working with thousands of pastors from all fifty states and several countries, we have concluded that a healthy pastoral workweek is in the range of forty-eight to fifty-two hours per week. In fact, experience has taught us that once a pastor hits fifty-two hours of work per week, the quality of work begins to significantly decline. This is not a recent discovery. Henry Ford understood this. In 1914, he changed his workforce from a nine-hour workday to an eight-hour workday. Then, in 1926, he adjusted from a six-day workweek to a five-day workweek. Ford believed the result would be greater production in shorter hours. He was right, and the forty-hour workweek was born. The lessons from Henry Ford should not be lost on the local church.

While it is true that no one can add time to their week, we can increase our capacity depth. Capacity depth fluctuates in different seasons of life. Depth increases when you are single, when you don't have children, and when you experience an empty nest. Be sensitive to your season of life. When a pastor has no children at home, spending three nights out a week might not be too much to ask. If a pastor has children at home, three nights a week away from home could bring his family to the breaking point. Financial realities also impact depth. While some may possess the financial means to hire help to clean the home and care for the yard, the majority of ministers have understood from the beginning that their calling could lead to financial challenges.

Finding Margin to Rest

In the history of sports, few coaches rival New England Patriots head coach Bill Belichick. When Hall-of-Fame quarterback Tom Brady and the Patriots overcame a twenty-five-point deficit in Super Bowl LI to defeat the Atlanta Falcons and capture their fifth Lombardi trophy, it was the stuff of legend. Perhaps only Vince Lombardi himself has a better résumé.

After the win, the city of Boston celebrated with yet another victory parade. Between the Celtics, Bruins, and Red Sox, the parade route is known by every man, woman, and child in New England. This particular year, during the concluding rally, Coach Belichick made a troubling statement for the entire world to hear. In an effort to explain why the Patriots have been so successful in the past and why they will continue to be successful in the future, Coach Belichick began to chant (actually scream), "No days off! No days off! No days off!" The cringeworthy chant went on for close to a minute until someone gathered the courage to pat the coach on the back and gently escort him away from the microphone. It didn't take a genius to read the faces of his coaching staff. I can only imagine the looks on the faces of the coaching staff spouses!

Sadly, "No days off" is too often the cry of the local church. The Bible clearly commands us to take the adequate time to rest. Our heavenly Father established a pattern of Sabbath when He rested on the seventh day. Jesus withdrew from the crowds to be alone (Mark 1:35). When I meet a pastor who tells me that there is no need for rest ("I'll rest one day in heaven!"), I gently ask, "If our heavenly Father took a day to rest, and yet you think you don't need Sabbath, who do you think you are?"

From the beginning of creation, the Lord established a rhythm to life. In Genesis 1–2, God creates the world and then rests. Why would God rest when He can't get tired? When the Lord rested, He established a pattern for all of creation. The Lord wasn't seeking physical or emotional rest. We are told in Genesis 2:2 that God rested because He was satisfied. He was able to lay down the work of creation because He was pleased with what He was doing. God structured His people's schedule to allow rest. In Exodus 16, the Lord gives the Israelites a day of rest by allowing one day to not gather manna. He promises His people that on the sixth day, there would be a double provision that wouldn't spoil. God granted rest. God included rest in the Ten Commandments when He commanded the Israelites, "Remember the Sabbath day, to keep it holy" (Ex. 20:8). Sabbath reminds us that life has a rhythm. Without rhythm, music is awkward and out of sync. It just doesn't flow. So, too, when we are devoid of rest, we lack the necessary rhythm to fully function. While many think of Sabbath as restrictive, its original intention was to be an expansive gift that centers us.

As leaders in the community of faith, you do need physical rest, but you need soul rest even more. Because our greatest need lies deep within our hurried souls, the antidote is not merely a plan for time management, a week at the beach, or a good night's sleep. The remedy for your weary soul is a person. Jesus does not say, "Come to church." He says, "Come to me." We do not find true rest in a program or principle. We find it in Jesus.

Spiritual transformation comes as we enter the rest of Jesus. We don't enter that rest by trying harder to generate spiritual transformation, but by throwing ourselves into the merciful arms of God. You can rest because of Jesus' work on the cross. You can rest because Jesus is manna from heaven. And you can rest because Jesus is the bread of life. Life management is ultimately more about gospel clarity than it is strategic management tools.

SELF-ASSESSMENT

On a scale of 1 to 5, how developed are you in the competency of life planning and management?

1	2	3	4	5
"I admit I am clueless in this competency."	"I know enough to know what I don't know."	"I can get by."	"I have a healthy skill set in this competency."	"I'm killing it in this area."

CHAPTER 15

MINISTRY MANAGEMENT

I joined the staff of Mitchell Road Presbyterian Church in Greenville, South Carolina, in 1988. I welcomed the opportunity to serve at Mitchell Road because it was an opportunity to serve under John Wood. I admired John for many reasons, not least his ability to clearly communicate the gospel. John had created a culture that encouraged me to try new things and, in some cases, fail, knowing I was secure in my position. He built a culture where risk was not only accepted but encouraged.

Under John's leadership, I did more than occasionally fail; I wrote the book on it. One time, to help create mission "experiences" on the church grounds (I was the youth and missions pastor), I brought in a helicopter from the Wycliffe base in North Carolina to give helicopter rides to anyone willing to wait in line. I brought in a petting zoo of African animals, including a jumbo-sized elephant that anyone could ride. Zebras, monkeys, and twelve-foot snakes mingled among the guests. It was incredible!

The failure came when the bill arrived. The elder board was not pleased that a pastor in his twenties had used church funds to create Adventure Land in the backyard of the church. But that freedom to fail led to greater risks, which led to greater opportunities.

The church had previously sent out an occasional mission team. That year we sent out six. I remember the weekend we reported on the trips to the church family. One of the elders who was furious with the mission conference bill and highly skeptical of sending out six mission teams approached me to apologize. With tears in his eyes, he confessed that he had not trusted me and had not believed the trips were possible. Two of his own children had participated in the trips, and they returned home transformed. All of this took place because of the amazing grace of the Lord Jesus, and because John trusted his staff.

Because God unceasingly works, we can regularly rest.

What I experienced under John's leadership is one of the five components of effective teams. Leaders must have the confidence to trust their team, the resolve to embrace reality, the passion to communicate vision, the wisdom to delegate, and the ability to provide perspective. These are essential tools in the toolbox of any ministry leader. And all of these can be found encompassed in the life of one leader, Nehemiah.

The Confidence to Trust

Trust in one another ultimately flows from trusting that our church, our ministry, our endeavor is God's, not ours. When we understand that our work is God's story, and that ultimately it is the name of Jesus we are working to uplift, we will give those around us the freedom to fail. Without trust, leaders will naturally become bottlenecks severely limiting the scope and span of service. Nehemiah led the Israelites in rebuilding Jerusalem's walls and gates in only fifty-two days because he trusted others to fulfill their commitments.

Trust accelerates delegation, which in turn accelerates meaningful ministry. Raise up those around you who are capable to serve, lead, and manage by giving them the opportunity to lead—and to fail.

Effective leaders know they don't need to work around the clock, because they trust that God is at work 24/7. Because God unceasingly works, we can regularly rest. Because Jesus perpetually reigns, you can establish life tempos that include rest. To ignore rest is to deny the sovereign grace of the Lord Jesus that He daily lavishes upon those who follow Him. Trust extended is first trust held. The foundation of effective ministry leadership is to remember that God is always at work. John 5:17 says, "Jesus answered them, 'My Father is working until now, and I am working.'"

This is an incredible promise bringing encouragement, comfort, and hope. God is unceasingly at work. Jesus is continually at work. The Holy Spirit is perpetually at work. Lamentations 3:22 reminds us that the Lord's loving kindnesses *never* cease. His compassions *never* fail. The eyes of the Lord are *always* on the land for which the Lord cares (Deut. 11:12). Last night, while you slept, the Lord, once again, was up all night. He never left His watch. He never slipped away to catch a nap. He didn't sleep because He is always at work (Ps. 121:1–5).

We can take this truth one step further. Because God is sovereign (Job 42:2; Ps. 115:3; 135:6; Luke 1:37), how much of His attention can He specifically give to you? All of His attention! And how often can He give you all of His attention? All of the time!

Here is a superlative truth that transforms how we lead our team: God is always able to give you His undivided attention, all of the time. He works 24/7 on every difficulty, each problem, and all challenges facing His people. This is a great comfort to any ministry leader. God is forever, unendingly, incessantly, relentlessly at work!

Embrace Reality

Far too often, we kill projects before they start because we failed to ask the right questions, carefully examine the task, and secure the necessary information. We accept the responsibility for an undertaking before knowing all the facts.

Nehemiah, after resting upon his arrival in Jerusalem, takes time to assess the wall project. In his midnight ride assessment (Neh. 2:12–15), he sees the situation firsthand. He inspects the walls and gates to see what shape they are in. Only after he gathers the facts and embraces reality does he publicly cast vision for the rebuilding project. This principle is one theme of the book of Proverbs (TLB):

> *Get the facts at any price, and hold on tightly to all the good sense you can get.* (Prov. 23:23)

> *What a shame—yes, how stupid!—to decide before knowing the facts!* (Prov. 18:13)

> *Only a simpleton believes everything he's told! A prudent man understands the need for proof.* (Prov. 14:15)

It is a mark of good leadership to understand expectations before agreeing to lead. Take time to research, conduct surveys, investigate demographics, and ask questions before accepting responsibility. When Nehemiah embraced the challenge to lead the rebuilding of Jerusalem's walls, he was embracing reality. The reality of the situation and the faith of Nehemiah were not in conflict. He understood the size of the project and the subsequent challenges. We should, too.

Passionately Communicate Vision

When Nehemiah prepares to cast vision for the rebuilding of the wall, he demonstrates one of the primary principles of effective ministry management: he helps people see what they can accomplish if they work together (Neh. 2:17–18). While we would anticipate a ninety-minute "State of the Union" speech, Nehemiah effectively casts a vision in three sentences by identifying with the people, explaining the situation, providing the "why," and getting to work:

> *Then I said to them, "You see the trouble we are in: Jerusalem lies in ruins, and its gates have been burned with fire. Come, let us rebuild the wall of Jerusalem, and we will no longer be in disgrace." I also told them about the gracious hand of my God upon me and what the king had said to me.*
>
> *They replied, "Let us start rebuilding." So they began this good work.* (NIV)

Too often, we set a low bar when inviting participation in a vision. Leaders should not feel bad that they ask too much, but that they ask too little. People like to be challenged to the near impossible. Legend has it that Sir Ernest Shackleton, when seeking recruits for his 1914 Antarctic expedition, posted an advertisement reading, "Men wanted for hazardous journey. Low wages, bitter cold, long hours of complete darkness. Safe return doubtful. Honor and recognition in event of success." He received more than enough interest.

In his first public words to the nation of Israel, Nehemiah immediately identifies with the people by stating, "You see the trouble we are in." Not you, but we. Nehemiah understood that guilt and shame are not a compelling motivation to do good work. Nehemiah did not begin by saying, "Okay, who screwed up? What a mess. Look what you've done. What were you doing under Ezra?" He does not criticize the previous rebuilding efforts. Hard work, when motivated by guilt, strangles you. Hard work, when motivated by the gospel, sanctifies you. Nehemiah knows that blame is not an effective motivational tool. Pushers say, "You." Leaders say, "We". You may have inherited a huge mess, a mess that you had no hand in creating. Effective leaders know that by climbing into the boat with those who created the mess, you have gained their respect, loyalty, and shared passion for transformative change.

Next, Nehemiah tells it like it is: the walls are in bad shape. Sometimes people need a dose of reality. Some dear friends of mine had a house that reeked of their dog. When I gently told them that their house smelled like a backed-up sewer that had been poured over a wet dog, they were in shock. They literally had no idea. They had lived in the midst of the stink for so long, they literally couldn't smell it. When you live with a bad situation long enough, you start ignoring it, becoming apathetic to reality. True leaders confront bad situations.

However, good leaders don't leave it there. After telling it like it is, they tell you what it can be. This is what Nehemiah did— "let us rebuild the wall of Jerusalem, and we will no longer be in disgrace"—and it motivated people to work. A vision devoid of reality is a pipe dream, but reality devoid of a vision is a nightmare. Give your people both.

The Wisdom of Delegation

While work is inherently good, the most effective leaders are not workaholics. The most productive leaders have learned to work hard without being in bondage to work. I so wish that as a young pastor I had understood that work is not a search for security but an expression of it. I wish that someone had taught me that delegation is the key to ministry management, and that the key to delegation is a combination of trust and humility.

Through delegation, trust, and humility, Nehemiah led Israel to rebuild the walls of Jerusalem in a mere fifty-two days (not that we should expect such quick results—sometimes our projects will take years, even decades). While it may be tempting to skip over a chapter filled with names you may be unable to pronounce, Nehemiah 3 is a lesson in delegation. It is organizational development at its best. Rather than thinking of rebuilding the Jerusalem walls and gates as one overwhelming project, Nehemiah breaks the project into forty-one sections, subsequently assigning teams to work on each one.

Delegation energizes others. It inspires a collective purpose. It means that the leader isn't clinging to power. Delegation demonstrates trust in others, as well as the leader's own security. It also means that you are willing to fail, as others may not work as effectively as you. Insecure, ego-driven managers who find their self-worth in work seldom delegate responsibility, effectively guaranteeing the failure of a project.

Delegation is effective only as others believe that their work is not about winning prestige, but about contributing to a grand outcome. The walls surrounding Jerusalem were approximately 2.5 miles around. Within the walls were a number of gates, including the Sheep Gate, Fountain Gate, Valley Gate, Water Gate (yes, a real gate), Fish Gate, Old Gate, Horse Gate, East Gate, and finally, in the south of the city wall, the Dung Gate. Certain gates held high prestige. The Sheep Gate was far and away the best gate, as it was located near the temple, where sacrifices would enter the city. Indisputably, at the bottom of the list was the Dung Gate. It doesn't take a rocket scientist to know what this was for. But if the Dung Gate was not repaired, the wall would be incomplete.

Nehemiah 3:14 tells the reader, "The Dung Gate was repaired by Malkijah son of Rekab, ruler of the district of Beth Hakkerem. He rebuilt it and put its doors with their bolts and bars in place" (NIV). Interestingly, Malkijah was an unlikely candidate to lead the team to complete the Dung Gate. His father was Rekab, ruler of the district of Beth Hakkerem, the highest point in the city of Jerusalem. In a time of battle, fighters would flee to Beth Hakkerem in order to fight from the highest and therefore the most strategic location in the city. In other words, Malkijah's dad was kind of a big deal. What if Malkijah had demanded a better gate in light of his father's standing in the community? Instead, the sense is that Malkijah—like the others—gladly contributed to the work.

Delegation is not about passing along undesirable tasks to others. Leaders do not delegate anything they are unwilling to do themselves. Rather, it is about inviting others to serve alongside you, and honoring them for their service. Everyone needs to find their place on the wall. Sometimes your place on the wall may be a sheep gate job, and other times it may be a dung gate job. Regardless, every role is honorable.

Provide Perspective

At PastorServe, one of our primary roles is to help pastors gain fresh perspective. At times, pastors are so deeply buried in conflict that they can't see the many ways in which the Lord has used them to bring gospel transformation to darkened hearts. Sometimes our job is to remind pastors of what they already know.

Recently, a pastor named Phil found himself in the midst of an enormous struggle that threatened the future of the church he had faithfully pastored for nearly a decade. The conflict came from the outside and was not of Phil's doing. He found himself discouraged, questioning the Lord's leading, wondering if it would have been better had he never planted the church. By God's providence (this is no coincidence), the night before I was to meet with Phil, I ran into a member of his congregation who recounted a story to me from ten years ago when Phil had deeply ministered to her. As a result of being so lovingly pastored, she was able to extend similar care to a close friend who had recently found herself in a parallel situation. The woman told me, "It was only because Phil cared for me and my family that God allowed me to care for my friend." The next morning, I was able to share that story with Phil. Not surprisingly, he broke down and wept. He had lost his perspective. One simple story brought renewed hope.

At PastorServe, we often meet with pastors who are in the midst of mighty struggles. We hear heartbreaking words like *downhearted, hurt, exhausted, angry, depressed, hopeless, despairing, frustrated, isolated, lonely, invalidated, dejected*. We have the privilege of reminding them of the truth of the gospel. We remind them that in Christ, they are loved, forgiven, treasured, justified, adopted, righteous, clean, hopeful, free, accepted, pardoned, secure, and blessed. In other words, we remind them of what they already know.

As a leader, provide perspective to those in your circle of influence. Remind others of God's daily provisions. Help people to raise their eyes above the fray of life to see the tender mercies of the Lord that are new every morning.

Like trust, we can only extend perspective if we have it. To maintain perspective in the midst of chaos (the rebuilding of a city), Nehemiah first went to the Lord in prayer. Nine times Nehemiah tells us that he sought the Lord in prayer. He understood that the effectiveness of his public leadership depended on God.

Leaders are ministry managers. They are organizational development practitioners. In *Resilient Ministry*, Bob Burns, Tasha Chapman, and Donald C. Guthrie wisely note that "leadership [is] seeking adaptive and constructive change, while management provides order and consistency to organizations."[17] Every component of leadership can be traced back to the level of trust we have that God is always at work. I wish someone had explained this to me in my early days of vocational ministry.

SELF-ASSESSMENT

On a scale of 1 to 5, how developed are you in the competency of ministry management?

1	2	3	4	5
"I admit I am clueless in this competency."	"I know enough to know what I don't know."	"I can get by."	"I have a healthy skill set in this competency."	"I'm killing it in this area."

CHAPTER 16

LEADERSHIP DEVELOPMENT

Many churches are in search of a leadership development shortcut. They want a simple, easy, painless program that results in qualified leadership. But leadership is risky, and embarking on biblical, thoughtful leadership development will take you deep into the bowels of the church. As one who has served hundreds of churches in crisis, the shortcuts are never, ever worth it. One ministry we provide at PastorServe is crisis care. When it comes to church crisis, the lowest common denominator we see most often is inadequate leadership development.

Healthy ministries simply must develop strong biblical leadership—there is no other way. And leadership training is not a weekend seminar. The most effective elder training courses commonly last anywhere from eighteen to twenty-four months.[18] Leadership training covers a combination of leadership principles, theology, shepherding, church polity (including church discipline), and the opportunity to practice hands-on pastoral care. In this chapter, I will focus on developing leaders in the local church, specifically elders (your church may call them something else).[19] Some readers may be leading in a different ministry context; these principles apply there, too.

Six Keys to Effective Leadership Development

The following six keys to leadership development in the local church are not *the* keys. To be sure, there are dozens of keys. I present these as central lessons I failed to understand at the outset of my pastoral ministry. Furthermore, these are not secrets. I do not believe there is a hidden leadership code in Scripture that only the brilliant few have unearthed. If that were the case, I would still be in search of number one. I do believe that these truths, if grasped and applied, will radically transform the leadership culture of your church.

1. Church leadership begins with church membership

There are countless stories of churches that launched with passion for the gospel, devotion to the Word of God, and commitment to the peace and purity of the church, only to drift from those things. I believe the answer lies early in the process, in receiving members who are not followers of Jesus. The following scenario is one I have encountered in other forms many, many times.

Bill is a well-known, Jesus-loving elder in the local church. Sadly, his youngest son, Ben, has been known to harbor addictions to alcohol, pornography, and sex. At some point, Ben comes to the church seeking membership. Though he is far from Jesus, every one of his older siblings have become members. This is a family rite of passage. The elders struggle, because this is a fellow elder's son, who they know is not a believer. Furthermore, Bill is blind to the rebellious nature of his son, believing him to be a devout follower of Jesus. The elders, not wanting to enter into a conflict with Bill, reluctantly receive Ben as a member. He may not love Jesus, but what harm could one person bring to the church? It's not a problem—for now.

Twenty years later, Ben is still a rebellious young man who has never fully surrendered his heart to Jesus. The pastor, knowing him not to be a believer, has spent countless hours with Ben. It is at that point that someone nominates Ben to the office of deacon. After twenty years, isn't it time he served as a deacon? While he won't be an elder, he will have a say in the church budget and the church facility. To the pastor's dismay, Ben is elected to the office of deacon. Ten years later, Ben is nominated to serve as an elder. He has been a church member for thirty years. He is well-known in the community. He is a successful businessman. Why shouldn't he be an elder? Soon after, Ben is installed as an elder. Now fifty, Ben has never been a Jesus follower. And yet, Ben is an elder, and five years later he is voted by his peers to serve as the chairman of the board.

This story is far from hypothetical. It has played out countless times in thousands of churches. The church is negatively impacted because an unbeliever came to lead the board. How? Because they were allowed to join the church when they clearly did not meet the biblical qualifications for church membership. If you are in a leadership position in your church and you compromise membership standards, you will likely be long gone before the repercussions of your shortsighted decision visibly affects the church. But understand this: while the impact of your decision might not be felt for twenty or thirty years, your compromise is presently eroding the foundation of the Lord's church.

2. Leadership should be decentralized

Ultimately, leadership and authority must be decentralized. There is a fine line between healthy visionary leadership and unhealthy centralized leadership. While the Lord does call leaders to provide visionary direction to a local church, they should exercise their gifts while sharing authority with a team of elders.

Decentralized leadership happens when we commit to recruiting and developing competent leaders we believe can pass us by. The strongest leaders are secure enough to find outstanding leaders and release them to lead. It is tempting to bypass the biblical process and appoint weak and easily manipulated leaders to shore up your control. If we hold someone up in the leadership cycle because we fear they will surpass us in leadership ability, we are saying that we matter more than the kingdom of God. Failing to raise up leaders because of insecurities weakens the local church. Secure, gospel-centered leadership finds great joy in watching others develop, grow, and succeed.

3. Leadership appointment is not leadership development

Too often, elders are placed into the highest office in the church because they lead successful businesses, are well respected, and are known to be substantial givers. While the Bible affirms the need to have elders who are respected in the community (1 Tim. 3:1) and not addicted to money (1 Tim. 3:3), there are no qualifications that mention leading in the marketplace. Furthermore, generosity in Scripture is judged by the percentage of one's giving rather than the amount (Mark 12:42–43).

Never appoint anyone into the role of elder because they are being "grandfathered" in. If someone relocates into your community who has served as a leader in a well-known church and they express a desire to immediately return to a position of local church leadership, insist that they go through the leadership track along with every other prospective leader. If a Fortune 500 CEO wants to serve as an elder, insist that they undergo the same training as the man or woman working in a factory line. First, the CEO will learn new things that were not taught in the Harvard MBA program, making him or her a more effective CEO. Second, no one will question the leadership training requirement if even the CEO has to go through it. Make no exceptions. If they are unwilling, they have demonstrated they lack the character required, anyhow.

4. Leadership is multi-dimensional

Leadership is far from one-dimensional. It is a three-legged stool comprising knowledge, experience, and skill. Stated another way, it requires a balance of knowing, being, and doing. Effective leaders know what to say (logos), how to say it (pathos), and how to carry themselves (ethos).

Leadership and management expert Peter Drucker has said there are three keys to a good hire: competency (they can do the job), character (they will do the job), and compatibility (they fit the team). Drucker's principles certainly apply to leaders in the church. Renaut's church wisely adds two to the list: calling and capacity.

Competency

Elders are called to lead the church, teach the Word, and judge doctrinal issues. An elder must not be a new believer (1 Tim. 3:6), lest they become conceited. They need to anticipate the repercussions of strategic decisions. Elders need to possess the theological acumen to identify and correct false teaching. They need to embrace the leadership competencies set forth in this book.

Character

When the Bible talks about the qualifications for elders, it focuses primarily on character (1 Tim. 3:1–8; Titus 1:5–9). The majority of the qualifications are relational. An elder is one who will shepherd, serve, and pastor the congregation. They faithfully pray for the sick and the lost. They freely and joyfully admit their brokenness, knowing that confessing their sin only magnifies the glory of Christ.

I remember when PastorServe consulted with a Florida church on the verge of hiring a lead pastor. A particular candidate had emerged who looked to be a home run. The staff, elder board, and church leaders were thrilled to have a high-caliber leader step into a leadership void. The church had asked me to travel to Florida to be a part of the final interview. Everyone was well aware that the final meeting would be more of a confirmation than an interview. When I arrived, I received a phone call from a close friend who happened to have crossed paths with the lead pastor candidate a decade earlier. He expressed that he had been reluctant to call, but he wanted to make sure I knew that the candidate had been fired ten years earlier for stealing from his church. He had misappropriated approximately $25,000. Because the funds were eventually returned, the elders of the church agreed to keep the theft internal and confidential.

No, I did not know. In fact, no one in the Florida church knew. After a lengthy discussion, the church board agreed that this was not a deal breaker, as long as the pastor would confess his sin, own what he had done, and share how the grace of God had impacted his life over the past decade. The night of the final interview, the leadership team demonstrated amazing grace to the candidate. After a number of questions revolving around preaching and outreach, he was asked to share a story about a time in his life when he went through a deep valley, and what he had learned through the experience. After a long pause, he said, "The most painful experience of my life was when I failed to qualify for nationals in debate my senior year of college." We honestly thought he was joking. We asked again. Has there been a hard experience in life, something that might have been caused by sin, that led you into a dark place, and how did the Lord demonstrate His grace and mold you more into His likeness through that circumstance? Again, the answer was college debate. We asked a third time. If it were a softball game, we lobbed a ball the size of a beach ball towards the plate. Anyone could hit this! The third time we asked, his countenance changed. It was immediately evident that he knew that we knew. Again, a long pause. This time he looked up and said, "I withdraw my name from consideration." And with that, he stood up and exited the room.

It was a heartbreaking night. It exposed a man who could not admit his brokenness, his sin, and his desperate need for Jesus. Godly character glorifies in weakness because it reveals the grace and mercy of Jesus (2 Cor. 11:16–31). A godly leader will exhibit humility and grace and will gladly testify to the goodness of the Lord in the life of a broken sinner.

Compatibility

An elder must fit on the leadership team. They must be able to work collaboratively with others. In many ways, a leadership team is like a jigsaw puzzle. Elders should fit well in the current elder context, both in personality, leadership, and ability. At PastorServe, we have worked with a number of churches that have been held hostage by one leader who is unwilling to play his or her role on the team.

They believe it is their calling to be the dissenting voice. If anyone believes that they have been called to play the antagonist role, they are delusional. One overbearing elder can bring an organization to a standstill. An elder needs to listen well, speak at appropriate times, and be both teachable and humble in times of disagreement.

Calling

Has the Holy Spirit prompted them to seek this position? An elder must sense in his or her heart a desire to lead and shepherd God's people (1 Tim. 3:1). This desire must also be affirmed and validated by others who are both observing and benefitting from this person's ministry. Furthermore, the spouse must be on board with the calling to the office of overseeing elder.

Capacity

Does this leader have the margin in their schedule to serve? As much as a person might want to serve, if they are on the road two hundred days a year, they are not in a place where they can effectively shepherd within a church. Even if an elder candidate meets the first four criteria, they must then have the personal margin of life to serve, as the duties of an elder require significant weekly planned commitments. Elder duties also regularly require spontaneous pastoral response. An elder must have the capacity and flexibility to handle both.

5. Leadership development is a perpetual cycle

Don't stop the leadership development process because the stable is full. For example, a leader makes an enormous mistake when, after recruiting and training six new elders, he or she shuts down the leadership development program. More times than I can count, I have listened to stories of competent, gifted, and called leaders who arrived in a local church "one year too late because the elders had already been selected."

Every church should continually train fresh new leadership. If you are conducting a two-year leadership development program, recruit a new cohort every year to begin the program. No one in your church should ever feel like they missed the window to enter into leadership training. My heart hurts when I visit a church twenty years after my last visit and find exactly the same leaders leading in exactly the same way. Keeping the leadership cycle open will invite continual classes of young, fresh, passionate leaders into the influential position of servant leader.

6. Leadership needs high EQ and CQ

Even first-class training programs can miss these critical principles: emotional and cultural intelligence. Though closely aligned, the two demand separate consideration.

Burns, Chapman, and Guthrie define and describe both of these terms in great detail in *Resilient Ministry*. They write, "Emotional intelligence [EQ] is the ability to manage one's own emotions pro-actively and to respond appropriately to the emotions of others."[20] It is a terrible irony that most pastors have been taught to exegete Scripture but not people. This is critical for leadership, discipleship, and conflict management.

Closely linked to EQ, cultural intelligence (CQ) can be de-fined as the ability to understand, acknowledge, and appreciate current contextual forces as well as the cultural background of others and oneself. It involves an awareness of regional, ethnic, and generational differences and the implications of these dif-ferences on one's worldview. Far too many leadership teams have been crippled by intellectual leaders who could not relate well to people. The best leaders are culturally astute, relationally sensitive, socially adept, and, above all, self-aware.

The call to serve as a local church leader is a call to equip, protect, love, serve, contribute, submit, pursue, steward, and sacrifice on behalf of the Lord's church. Leadership development is a process by which potential candidates are instructed in doctrine (orthodoxy) and practice (orthopraxy)—head, heart, and hands—so they can connect the Bible to the everyday details of their lives and their flock.

SELF-ASSESSMENT

On a scale of 1 to 5, how developed are you in the competency of leadership development?

1	2	3	4	5
"I admit I am clueless in this competency."	"I know enough to know what I don't know."	"I can get by."	"I have a healthy skill set in this competency."	"I'm killing it in this area."

PART IV DISCUSSION QUESTIONS

1. On a scale of one to five (five being mastery), how developed are you in the core competency of leading the body of believers?

2. Of the sub-competencies (leadership, life planning and management, ministry management, leadership development), which is your strongest? Which is your weakest?

3. What is one way you can lean into your strongest sub-competencies?

4. What is a practice you can implement this week to grow in your weakest sub-competencies?

5. Who could you partner with to cover your weaknesses and minister more effectively together?

PART V

Serve the Body
of Believers

CHAPTER 17

BUILDING BIBLICAL COMMUNITY

In the spring of 1940, during the apex of World War II, Hitler's panzer divisions advanced on the Allied soldiers, trapping them in Dunkirk, France. With the harbor and ocean behind them, and the force of Hitler before them, all seemed lost. The majority of Belgian and Dutch troops had already surrendered, and 225,000 British soldiers and another 110,000 French and Allied soldiers faced certain capture or death. The British Royal Navy had enough ships available to rescue 17,000 soldiers from the French beach. The remaining 320,000 soldiers would face the fury of an unmerciful Hitler. Churchill told the House of Commons to brace for hard tidings.

Winston Churchill called what followed "Operation Dynamo." In nine days, from May 27 to June 4, as the world watched in amazement, a ragtag fleet of more than nine hundred merchant marine vessels, fishing boats, sailboats, pleasure crafts, rowboats, and lifeboats—all captained by civilians—made their way to Dunkirk and rescued 338,226 Allied soldiers. Every English floating vessel was called into duty. If the owners could not be contacted, available ships were simply commandeered for use in the rescue operation. The fleet would come to be known as the "Little Ships of Dunkirk." It remains one of the most beautiful demonstrations of community that the world has ever witnessed.

As the miraculous rescue concluded, England was reinvigorated by the success of Operation Dynamo. Upon the last soldier's rescue, Churchill stood before the House of Commons on June 4, 1940, and said, "We shall fight on the beaches, we shall fight on the landing grounds, we shall fight in the fields and in the streets, we shall fight in the hills; we shall never surrender."[21] Churchill's words are remembered as one of the greatest speeches of the twentieth century.

The story of Dunkirk moves me because it is a picture of the kingdom of God, a ragtag band of followers who have been captured by Christ reaching out to serve and save others who remain in the same waters from which we were rescued. Dunkirk is a story of community and the need for connection, because everyone comes to a point in life when they need the intervention of others to rescue them from the coming darkness. Dunkirk is a story of what can be accomplished when we join together to attempt the impossible.

First Corinthians 12 reminds the church that we are all a part of the body of Christ. If one suffers, we all suffer. When one part is honored, we all rejoice. Community was never intended to be a program in the local church. Participation in a small group and attending the annual church picnic do not get close to the biblical ideal (though I love a good picnic). Community is and always has been designed to be a core value of every church and every believer. The local church is defined as the visible community of believers.

The Biblical Basis for Community

Biblical community begins with the basic understanding that everyone, including ministry leaders, were created for community. The church is a gathering of Christians who have been called from isolation into authentic biblical community. Christian community is the gathering of believers, not only in body but also in heart. While there are several expressions of biblical community, I want to focus in this chapter on small groups.[22]

Believers gathering in smaller communities to share life together began in the Old Testament. There were five divisions within the nation of Israel: the nation, the tribe (the twelve tribes of Israel), the clan (in the book of Exodus we are told there were fifty-seven clans among the twelve tribes), the household (the extended family), and the family. The home played a key role in Jewish culture. The house church became a natural expression of this emphasis.

The supreme example of biblical small-group community comes from Jesus and His twelve disciples. Jesus spent the majority of His time with His band of brothers. They traveled together, ate together, experienced hardship together, and lived life together in a real-life leadership training lab. Relationships, not organizations, were central to Jesus' method of reaching the world with the good news. In this community, far from a formal academic experience, Jesus taught and modeled spiritual truths and attitudes. In community Jesus equipped His disciples to carry on the work of the gospel.

Jesus' model of community was lived out in the early church, especially in the home. Acts 2:46–47 indicates that gathering in homes was a daily occurence:

And day by day, attending the temple together and breaking bread in their homes, they received their food with glad and generous hearts, praising God and having favor with all the people. And the Lord added to their number day by day those who were being saved.

While meetings in the temple court were a significant part of the early church, gathering in homes was, too. It's worth noting that the house church did not emerge as a result of persecution. As persecution increased, the house church grew in significance, but the need for small gatherings of believers has always been the norm.

In the fourth century, Christians began to build church buildings. As the popularity of the building gradually increased, the house church began to slowly diminish. By AD 1250, the Gothic temple had reached its height of popularity. At that time, a theological error began to be spread, one alive and well today: that church is not the people but the building. And yet, nowhere in Scripture or the writings of the early church fathers is the church referred to as a structure—except as a metaphor for referring to people! And nowhere in Scripture are we commanded to bring members of our broader community into a structure referred to as the church. In fact, the command to believers is to take the church into our community. The church needs to be taken where believers work, live, eat, and play. The church needs to be taken to the arts, the business community, and the medical world. The church needs to be carried into education, government, and media. The church needs to touch every fragment and segment of our community.

I believe that regularly gathering together both in a larger community worship service as well as a house gathering is the ideal. Gathering together is an opportunity to celebrate the sacraments of baptism and the Lord's Supper, as well as hear the Word preached. Gathering with a larger community allows for celebration, inspiration, and emotional connection, while gathering with a smaller community will emphasize devotion, mission, and relational connection. Large gatherings are important, but most of the Christian life is lived in small gatherings and day-to-day community. There are more than one hundred "one another" instructions given to believers in the New Testament—love one another, be devoted to one another, carry one another's burdens, etc.—that simply cannot be lived out in a large group setting devoid of personal relationships. When Hebrews 10:24–25 encourages us to "spur one another on toward love and good deeds" by "meeting together," it means more than a Sunday morning worship service. It means finding fellowship in community throughout the week.

The Assault on Authentic Biblical Community

Social media alone cannot replace community. While digital interaction can augment community, it is not a replacement. It is a growing trend for those in isolation to define their online e-community as their church, but this is a stretch. Your Twitter, Instagram, and TikTok followers and Facebook friends cannot be your sustained biblical community because they are, in a literal sense, virtual.

A shrinking percentage of people within the United States are connected to a church community. Less than 20 percent attend worship services, and those who self-identify as "active" attend on average 1.9 times per month. To have five hundred attend an average weekend service, more than one thousand people would need to call your church home. While the COVID-19 pandemic made attending church from our living room the norm for a season, the long-term approach of watching your favorite preacher online does not qualify as sustainable biblical community. The coronavirus pandemic set several dangerous precedents if they are adopted as a long-term strategy. For example, a resident of California erroneously may consider himself to be an active member of a New York church community because he watches the worship service live every week. But ask anyone in that church if they know him.

To be engaged in community means opening one's heart to fellow sojourners. Not surprisingly, to be in community means that we have something in common. The words *common*, *community*, *communication*, and *communion* all share the same root. What we have in common is Jesus Christ. Because we have Jesus Christ in common, we minister to one another simply by being together. That is what we mean in the Apostle's Creed when we say "the communion of saints." We don't have to have a Bible study to have community. There is community when we gather with believers for a game of softball. No pre-game prayer is needed to sanctify the event.

For a number of years, the Lord flung open doors for me to minister to people who were engaged in cults. I was able to engage in hundreds of conversations with those who were often living under indescribable oppression. At the outset, I wrongly believed that by demonstrating the error of their theology, I could help them see the truth. I worked to master a carefully crafted biblical response to every argument that might be thrown my way. And yet, after engaging in theological debates with a number of people, I had an insight that changed the way I approach people trapped in a cult. Literally no one I met joined the cult because they were in search of truth and found it in their cult. People join cults because they are in search of community. People join cults because someone invited them into a place where they felt loved, accepted, and valued. When you are isolated, lonely, desperate for connection, and in search of community, you generally don't care what the other person believes, as long as that person genuinely receives you into their group.

While you may be passionate about biblical theology (as am I), the primary calling card of your church must be authentic community. The majority of people who are in search of a local church are generally shopping for church as a social association and not a theological institution. Good theology and good community go hand in hand.

The Disappointment of Community

There is inevitable heartache that comes with community. Real life and real community lead inescapably to conflict. But the certain pain is no excuse to avoid community. Rick Warren, summarizing a key theme of Dietrich Bonhoeffer's classic on fellowship, *Life Together*, writes, "Disillusionment with our local church is a good thing because it destroys our false expectations of perfection. The sooner we give up the illusion that a church must be perfect in order to love it, the sooner we quit pretending and start admitting we're all imperfect and need grace. This is the beginning of real community."[23] When we don't acknowledge and admit our imperfection, we play the church game. We come to church lonely, isolated, and afraid of being discovered. We put a smile on our face, sit through worship and small groups, and go home unchanged to our prisons of emotional isolation. The remedy is to bring our whole life to church—our pain, brokenness, hopes, fear, shame, and yes, even our joys.

Missional living in community is unquestionably difficult.

Admittedly, doing life together is messy, hard, and painful. Living in community involves risk.

But you know what's harder? Living without community. Isolation means being unknown. Community means living life fully known. Isolation protects the façade of the frontstage. Community allows us to be known on the backstage of real life. Isolation sees only above the waterline. Authentic biblical community looks below the waterline.

As I look back on my journey, there are certain seasons I couldn't imagine going through without community. When my wife's younger brother died after battling cancer for nearly two decades, we needed community. When my wife and I adopted Paige and Allie, we needed community. When both of my parents were called home to be with Jesus, we needed community. The list goes on and on. When our brokenness is before us, we need community. The need for community is birthed out of the impossibility of living life to the fullest in isolation. Community leads to life.

We must intentionally, passionately fight for the belief that we were created for community. We long to belong. We want to be wanted. Deep in our hearts we all yearn for release from isolation. We're all interconnected as the body of Christ, which means that it is not possible to be freestanding, isolated entities. It's not possible to survive apart from one another.

SELF-ASSESSMENT

On a scale of 1 to 5, how developed are you in the competency of building biblical community?

1	2	3	4	5
"I admit I am clueless in this competency."	"I know enough to know what I don't know."	"I can get by."	"I have a healthy skill set in this competency."	"I'm killing it in this area."

CHAPTER 18

DISCIPLE-MAKING

As an American, I owe a deep debt of gratitude to each member of the armed services. I profoundly respect the Army, Navy, Air Force, Marines and Coast Guard. Both my father and my father-in-law served in the United States Navy. And while I have the highest respect for each of the military special forces, my admiration is the greatest for the Navy SEALs. I have long been drawn to their heroic acts of bravery and sacrifice.

The mission of the Navy SEALs is to "Man, Train, Equip, Deploy and Sustain NSW Forces for operations and activities abroad, in support of Combatant Commanders and U.S. National Interests."[24] Stated another way, SEAL forces conduct the most important missions in defense of our country and for freedom everywhere. If you are having a day in which you need a little inspiration to get off the couch, read the SEAL creed. Here are a few statements from it:

> In times of war or uncertainty there is a special breed of warrior ready to answer our Nation's call. Common citizens with uncommon desire to succeed. . . . I am that warrior. . . .

> ... I humbly serve as a guardian to my fellow Americans always ready to defend those who are unable to defend themselves. I do not advertise the nature of my work, nor seek recognition for my actions....
>
> I serve with honor on and off the battlefield. The ability to control my emotions and my actions, regardless of circumstance, sets me apart from others. Uncompromising integrity is my standard....
>
> ... I lead by example in all situations.[25]

Thank God for these valiant warriors who answer this call. SEALs have an unparalleled demanding process to recruit, prepare, equip, and deploy. Perhaps one reason I am drawn to the SEAL culture is that so much of what embodies their mission is grounded in the Holy Scriptures.

Mobilizing Followers of Jesus

As followers of Jesus, we too are commanded to recruit, prepare, equip, and deploy. Recruiting is the call of Jesus to share the good news. To prepare and equip is the process of training and outfitting disciples. It is the command to faithfully teach the truths of the gospel. During this preparation time, we train men and women to be disciples of Jesus. We model what it means to follow Jesus. Equipping involves outfitting followers of Jesus with the proper tools to fulfill their mission. In discipleship, both are essential. Can you imagine a Navy SEAL team being trained and then deployed before being outfitted with the proper clothing, communications tools, and weapons to fulfill the mission? To deploy is the call to mission. Each of these plays a significant role in the development of devoted followers of Jesus.

In *Growing True Disciples*, George Barna states,

> Offering programs is not the issue. We discovered that surprisingly few churches have a well-conceived model of discipleship that they implement. The result is that churches feel they have fulfilled their obligation if they provide a broad menu of courses, events, and other experiences, but such a well-intentioned but disjointed approach leaves people confused and imbalanced.[26]

The Bible expects all Christians—and especially the leaders of Christ's church—to focus on spiritual growth (John 14:23, 1 Tim. 4:7,16). As leaders, our responsibility is to help people identify where they are, where they need to go, and how to get there. And we don't need to complicate it. Discipleship is simply a synonym for Christian living. Eugene Peterson says that "discipleship is a process of paying more and more attention to God's righteousness and less and less attention to our own."[27] How are we helping our parishioners do that?

Most believers desire to grow spiritually but lack the necessary disciplines and knowledge to do so. When ill-equipped to mature in their walk with the Lord, many feel static, confused, and defeated. I have far too many stories of people who were deployed to serve the Lord without any reproducible tools, even though the most basic tools can easily be taught to any willing believer. Are you doing everything you can to help people mature?

Taking Up the Cross

One of the most common ways leaders stunt their church's maturity is by encouraging immaturity. I am thinking specifically of how we preach the gospel.

I wonder if we often soft-sell the gospel for fear that a radical call to a resolute commitment will turn people away from surrendering their life to Jesus. In the Gospel of Mark, all believers are called to radically live as wholly devoted followers. When we share Jesus with others, are we consistently presenting a faithful picture of Jesus' call to discipleship? This is what Jesus calls your church to:

> *Then he called the crowd to him along with his disciples and said: "Whoever wants to be my disciple must deny themselves and take up their cross and follow me. For whoever wants to save their life will lose it, but whoever loses their life for me and for the gospel will save it. What good is it for someone to gain the whole world, yet forfeit their soul?"* (Mark 8:34–36)

A disciple is someone who has heard the call of Jesus and responded by repenting (saying no to oneself and yes to Jesus), believing the gospel, and following Him. Denying means total abandonment of self-reliance and total acknowledgment of Jesus-dependence. Leaders build the bridge between believing the call of the gospel and living it out. Discipleship is the long, often painful process of moving followers of Jesus from independence to complete and utter dependence upon Jesus.

What is so interesting about the call of Jesus to His disciples is that "taking up your cross" is not a Jewish metaphor. The picture is that of a condemned man going to die with a cross on his back. Writing in *The Cost of Discipleship*, Dietrich Bonhoeffer reminds the reader,

> The cross is laid on every Christian.... As we embark upon discipleship we surrender ourselves to Christ in union with His death—we give over our lives to death. Thus it begins; the cross is not the terrible end to an otherwise god-fearing and happy life, but it meets us at the beginning of our communion with Christ. When Christ calls a man, He bids him come and die.[28]

As leaders, we cannot be found guilty of perpetuating the lie that every hardship is suffering for Christ. Sickness, cancer, and a host of other difficulties this life throws at us are not examples of taking up the cross of Jesus. Rather, taking up our cross is reflected in difficulties that have come about as a result of following Jesus. Did you lose your job because your company downsized? That is not bearing your cross. Did you lose your job because you refused to compromise ethical behavior to make a sale? That is bearing the cross of Jesus. And taking up the cross is not only the destiny of Jesus, it is the destiny of every believer.

Mark 8:35 is a great paradox, which, in the words of G. K. Chesterton, is a truth standing on its head calling out for attention: "For whoever wants to save his life will lose it, but whoever loses his life for me and for the gospel will save it" (NIV). In the kingdom of God, losing means saving, last is first, less is more, and the shame of the cross is the glory of God. This is the message we need to proclaim to our churches, regardless of the results. Bonhoeffer said, "So many people come to church with a genuine desire to hear what we have to say, yet they are always going back home with the uncomfortable feeling that we are making it too difficult for them to come to Jesus."[29] Leaders are called to faithfully preach the gospel and then trust the Holy Spirit to bring results.

Recruit, Prepare, Equip, Deploy

You can understand most of the book of Acts as occurring somewhere on this continuum of recruiting, preparing, equipping, or deploying. In one sense, Jesus recruits His apostles for His mission at Acts 1:8: "But you will receive power when the Holy Spirit comes on you; and you will be my witnesses in Jerusalem, and in all Judea and Samaria, and to the end of the earth." And then, with every trip to the synagogue, the streets, or across a sea, the apostles were in the business of recruiting more followers. How much recruiting is your church doing? Most of the decisions the apostles made were recruiting ones; how much can that be said of your church?

Preparation and equipping cannot happen without recruits, but recruiting is fruitless without preparation and equipping. If you read the Gospels and Acts back to back, you will see that Jesus was actually preparing and equipping the disciples for the job He would eventually recruit them for, especially through modeling gospel ministry for them.

For example, look at the parallels between one of Jesus' healing stories in Mark and one of Peter's in Acts:

Jesus

He [Jesus] put them all outside and took the child's father and mother and those who were with him and went in where the child was. Taking her by the hand he said to her, "Talitha cumi," which means, "Little girl, I say to you, arise." And immediately the girl got up and began walking (for she was twelve years of age), and they were immediately overcome with amazement. And he strictly charged them that no one should know this, and told them to give her something to eat. (Mark 5:40–43)

Peter

But Peter put them all outside, and knelt down and prayed; and turning to the body he said, "Tabitha, arise." And she opened her eyes, and when she saw Peter she sat up. And he gave her his hand and raised her up. Then, calling the saints and widows, he presented her alive. And it became known throughout all Joppa, and many believed in the Lord. (Acts 9:40–42)

Peter was clearly prepared and equipped under the tutelage of Jesus. The same is true even of Paul, mysteriously so, since he didn't walk with Jesus until after His ascension. But it was Paul who wrote, "Be imitators of me, as I am of Christ" (1 Cor. 11:1). The biblical model of preparation and equipping is primarily mentorship.

Personally, the greatest period of training for ministry took place when I was discipled by Jerry Root, a well-loved professor at Wheaton College. At the time, Jerry was the college pastor at the College Church in Wheaton, and I was a student at Wheaton. During my sophomore year, I began stopping by Jerry's office regularly. I loved being around a man who so passionately loved Jesus. Jerry would sit with me and read the Scriptures and then help me understand the intent of the author. Occasionally, Jerry would read an original poem he had just written. Other times found us discussing a passage from the writings of Lewis or Tolkien. Before beginning my senior year at Wheaton, three significant things took place. Most importantly, I became engaged to Sally, who would later become my wife. Second, I was hired as a youth intern at College Church. I was privileged to have an office right down the hall from Jerry, which allowed me to interact with him daily. And third, Jerry and his wife, Claudia, asked me to live in their home.

Discipleship goes to another level when you move in with someone. Living in the Root home taught me more about marriage and life than I could have learned from reading a hundred books. Jerry and Claudia never put on a show because I was around. They never spoke in hushed voices as I passed by. I watched them raise their children. I listened to them argue (seldom, but usually revolving around Jerry's insistence that he play semi-professional football). I listened to them pray. I listened as they struggled with finances. While there were few times of intentional conversations in the home, there were countless casual interactions that taught me a great deal about life. I learned more standing in the kitchen talking with Jerry while he enjoyed a late-night snack than I did in several of my best college classes. When I married Sally in 1983, our marriage was stronger because of the time I had spent with Jerry and Claudia in their Wheaton home. I will forever be grateful to Jerry for preparing and equipping me for marriage, ministry, and simply loving Jesus.

When a soldier has been recruited, prepared through extensive training, and equipped with the proper tools, it is time to deploy. In deployment, the tools must match the mission. Peter had been trained and equipped during his years of walking and living with Jesus. In Acts 1:8, Jesus deployed Peter and the rest of the disciples by instructing them to be His witnesses in Jerusalem, Judea, Samaria, and unto the uttermost parts of the earth. So too, followers of Jesus must be deployed to take the message of Jesus to a lost and dying world.

As a commanding officer feels the weight of responsibility, so too we pastors feel a weight of responsibility for disciples under our care. But sadly, in some cases, it can become the ultimate thing. There is tremendous danger when we base our self-worth on the life and actions of those under our care. It is far too easy to blame ourselves when someone in whom we have invested a part of our life falls morally. Personally, I have been there many times. Each time I am reminded that the weight of discipleship ultimately rests at the foot of the cross of Jesus Christ. On the cross, Jesus died for my guilt, shame, anxiety, fear, and misplaced responsibility.

Discipleship is the call of the gospel. Discipleship is the invitation from Jesus to devote all of life to a higher purpose, advancing the message of the kingdom of God. Nowhere in the Scriptures is discipling others assigned exclusively to pastors. Every follower of Jesus is called to be both a disciple and a disciple-maker. Are you making disciples who make disciples?

SELF-ASSESSMENT

On a scale of 1 to 5, how developed are you in the competency of disciple-making?

1	2	3	4	5
"I admit I am clueless in this competency."	"I know enough to know what I don't know."	"I can get by."	"I have a healthy skill set in this competency."	"I'm killing it in this area."

CHAPTER 19

SHEPHERDING

"So I exhort the elders among you . . . shepherd the flock of God" (1 Peter 5:1–2). This is the pastor and elder's very job description. The church growth movement (more on this in chapter 22) emphasizes the need to adjust the role of the pastor from shepherd to rancher as the church outgrows the ability of one person to effectively attend to the people under his or her care. While I appreciate the need to restructure an organization to effectively provide care, redefining the pastor's role from shepherd to CEO is thoroughly unbiblical. Even Paul, who had the oversight of multiple congregations and the mind of a Fortune 500 CEO, shepherded the Ephesian church with many tears (Acts 20:19). In speaking about the Thessalonians, Paul says, "But we were gentle among you, like a nursing mother taking care of her own children. So, being affectionately desirous of you, we were ready to share with you not only the gospel of God but also our own selves, because you had become very dear to us" (1 Thess. 2:7–8).

The primary way God shepherds His people is through human shepherds. Moses was a shepherd called to shepherd God's people (Ps. 77:20). David was a shepherd called to shepherd God's people. And as God's chosen people struggled to follow the Lord, they were promised a Shepherd among shepherds who would feed them with knowledge and understanding (Ezek. 34:23–24; Jer. 3:15). That Great Shepherd, of course, is Jesus.

Despite a culture that calls the pastor to seek bigger, better, updated, streamlined programs (which is not necessarily negative), Jesus shows that the primary call of the pastor is to be a servant. Jesus didn't come with a massive marketing campaign, a killer social media presence, and a designer wardrobe. He demonstrated that true leadership has nothing to do with titles or position, but with service. The opposite of servant leadership is narcissism. People who talk about themselves incessantly. People with a stormy, heavy presence. People who don't notice, can't be corrected, and can't be bothered.

Jesus is the counter to the modern-day celebrity pastor who looks for every opportunity for self-promotion. When certain followers looked for every opportunity to make Jesus famous (John 7:1–9), our Lord's priority was to humbly serve. As the ultimate servant leader, though He is above us, He humbled Himself and subjected Himself to a human life and ultimately death on a cross. Jesus served you and me by dying for you and me.

As a pastor, you are called to minister in the way of Jesus. I want to offer three ways of doing that: providing hope through reminding, care through listening, and empathy through presence, especially care through listening. Staying close to these words will demonstrate that you have deep affection for the flock under your care.

Hope through Reminding

As a pastor, you know this, but sometimes the job of a shepherd is to teach. And other times it is the job of a shepherd to gently remind others of what they already know. In Titus 3:1, Peter instructs Titus to "remind them to . . ." In other words, this isn't going to be anything new. I'm simply here to remind you of what you already know. Unquestionably, your church is filled with many in the midst of mighty struggles. Many are downhearted, hurt, exhausted, angry, depressed, isolated, lonely, and rejected.

> We are called to be confident about the truth and dare people to believe it.

As spiritual leaders, we have the privilege of reminding them of the truth of the gospel. We are to carry that good news with us constantly as a healing balm. We remind them that in Christ, they are loved, forgiven, treasured, justified, adopted, righteous, clean, hopeful, free, accepted, pardoned, secure, and blessed. In other words, we remind them of what they already know.

The Lord brings people into your path daily. Sometimes you plan those encounters; others are unexpected divine appointments. In every instance, look for opportunities to remind others of the goodness and kindness of God.

Care through Listening

As spiritual leaders, our job is not to fix anyone. Our job is to voice and embody the gospel. We are called to be confident about the truth and dare people to believe it. One of the most effective things a pastor can do to shepherd his or her people is to listen. Personally, I came out of seminary feeling prepared to do far more talking than listening. I felt tremendous pressure to have good answers when confronted with difficult life situations. After all, I had just spent a small fortune, and anyone could sit and listen. I needed to give answers! I have since learned otherwise.

The majority of people who approach a pastor for counsel are not looking for a CEO to restructure their life. Rather, they are looking for a shepherd to listen to their story and process *with* them as they consider next steps. Effective counseling begins with active listening, which means we learn to listen from the inside out, discerning facts and feelings. I so wish that early on in my ministry, someone had trained me in the art of listening and asking the right questions. I wish I had learned to answer only after I had listened (Prov. 18:2). Where are they hurting? What are they celebrating? Leaders listen skillfully, identifying another's feelings and focus. People long for someone, anyone, to listen to them tell their story. The best leaders are the best listeners. Here are ten tools that will enhance coaching, counseling, and general communication.

> People who approach a pastor for counsel are not looking for a CEO to restructure their life.

1. Be aware of filters

Filters are events and resulting emotions from our own past that cause us to define things ahead of time. The best communicators regularly take inventory of their filters. Possible filters might include a past experience with a similar challenge, carrying a personal agenda, personal fatigue, coming into the counseling experience with a predetermined conclusion, and personal bias. The best listeners are aware of their own perspective and story. They acknowledge intentions, assumptions, emotions, values, loyalties, fears, needs, wants, and triggers. No one is 100 percent unbiased in any conversation. Admitting this is a major step in active listening.

2. Be aware of the difference between counseling and consulting

When a counselor shifts to consultant and begins to offer a solution, it generally communicates that they have no further interest in listening. Counseling conversations are fully interactive mutual conversations. They are not a didactic monologue but a collaborative dialogue. Counseling is a process of mutual exploration and discovery. When you are primarily directive in a counseling context, it has the feeling of a parent speaking to a child. If the majority of the counselor's statements begin with, "I think you should" or "I would strongly advise you to," it is demeaning to the counselee. Beginning reflections with, "Let's think about . . ." and "Let's unpack that last statement" will encourage thoughtful interaction. If a clear solution presents itself, gently share what might work in this situation.

3. Ask helpful questions

The most effective conversations begin with asking good, nonjudgmental questions. (Aim to be curious, not indicting.) I encourage beginning questions that begin with *what, when, who,* and *how.* For example, "What was the process you went through to . . .," "When did you decide to . . .," "Who else do you go to when . . .," "How did you feel when . . ."

When we begin questions with *why*, it generally puts people on the defensive. "Why are you always so late?" and "What are the reasons you find it hard to get to work on time?" are the exact same question asked in a very different manner. While the first question would often raise a person's defenses, the second question, while direct, invites a thoughtful response. When someone is facing a challenge, I suggest asking questions like:

- How great is your concern about the present challenge?

- Who is affected by this issue other than you?

- What action steps have you taken so far?

- What obstacles will need to be overcome on the way?

- What is really the issue here? What is the bottom line?

- What are the alternatives, large or small, complete and partial solutions?

- What would you do if you could start again with a clean slate?

- What are your criteria and measurements for success?

- Who needs to know your plans?

- What support do you need and from whom?

- Is there anything else you want to talk about?

4. Probe

Probing is another form of asking effective questions. There are closed probes and open probes. In a closed probe, questions are asked that encourage a yes or no response or a specific answer—for example, "Did you sleep well last night?" or "How much sleep did you get last night?"

An open probe encourages elaboration. It is an open-ended question that invites a thoughtful response:

- Tell me how you are doing with this project.

- What emotions did you experience when there was little to no response to your invitation?

- What are you and your spouse doing to cope in this busy season?

A closed probe is like fishing with a hook, whereas an open probe is like fishing with a net. If you are trying to focus in upon one specific issue, then a closed probe can be helpful. If your singular goal is to gather information, then by all means use open probes. Men will typically use three times as many closed probes as open probes. If men are not careful and they string several closed probes together, conversation can begin to feel like an attorney taking a deposition. Ask questions that allow people to share genuinely from the depths of their heart.

5. Be aware of nonverbal communication

Communication is more than just words. Does your body posture communicate care and concern? Crossed arms express judgment, whereas open arms are inviting. An erect posture shows you are engaged, while slumping in your chair says you'd rather be somewhere else. Tone of voice conveys even more. The same question in a different tone can either communicate compassion or condemnation. Changing even one point of inflection can project care or criticism.

6. Acknowledge

Acknowledging simply affirms to the listener that you are actively engaged in the conversation. Simple statements such as, "Hmmm, I see. OK, yes. I understand" tell the counselee that you are present and involved in what he or she is saying. A slight nod of the head communicates that you are listening and have not allowed your mind to drift to last night's football game.

7. Reflect

In counseling as in the drive-thru lane, reflecting is your bread and butter. After you place an order, the restaurant employee will always repeat it back to ensure its accuracy. You should do the same as a counselor. By briefly restating what someone has just said, you minimize miscommunication and misunderstanding, and you help your counselee feel understood. Only then can you truly help them. Reflecting is not a natural skill but is developed over time.

8. Respect

It helps no one when we make irrelevant contemptuous statements. We must be careful to not discount ("Oh, everybody struggles with that"), ridicule ("Well, congratulations, you have the spiritual gift of alienation"), criticize ("Well, that was a short-sighted decision"), or patronize ("Well, personally, I don't feel that way—I love my wife"). When we disrespect others, honest communication is squelched. All communication is built on a foundation of honor and respect.

9. Encourage self-disclosure

Self-disclosure occurs when you, the listener, briefly share a personal story that can shed light on the discussion. This is a dangerous but necessary component of active listening. These statements must be very brief, as they are really just a way of entering into the counselee's story through one of your own. Self-disclosure is not a license to launch into telling mode. Don't hijack their story. It is a simple relevant story or observation that communicates that you can empathize. Before self-disclosing, always seek the permission of the other person. "Would you be okay if I shared a short story from my own life that I believe could bring some clarity to your current situation?"

10. Summarize

Encapsulate the session in a couple of closing statements. This assures the counselee that you were actively listening and truly understand them—and that you both agree about any next steps. An effective summary should take no more than thirty seconds.

Empathy through Presence

Barbara was called to go to the home of a close friend whose husband had unexpectedly passed away only hours before. As she left the church, she came into my office and broke down in tears. She said, "I don't know why I am going! I have nothing to say. Everyone there knows the Bible so much better than me." Two hours later, she returned in worse shape than before. She again broke down. "Everyone there knew exactly what to say. I couldn't think of anything. I just sat there, tears streaming down my face as I hurt for my friend. I feel like a fool."

The next day, Barbara's phone rang. It was the friend, asking Barbara to return to her home. She said, "Out of all the women who were here throughout the day, I felt like you were the only one who genuinely entered into my pain." Barbara hadn't said one word. Sometimes the most effective method of empathy is absolute silence.

The best counseling session in the Bible is recorded in Job 2. After Job loses everything, three friends gather to comfort him. Verses 12 and 13 tell us that the friends weep, tear their clothes, and sprinkle dust on their heads. They sit with Job for seven days and nights and don't say one word, because they saw the depth of his suffering. And then they opened their mouths and blew it! Sometimes the most powerful communication is our presence.

In summary, the main task of pastoring a church is shepherding the people. Pastor with the heart of a compassionate, patient, listening shepherd. In doing so, you will reflect the heart of the Chief Shepherd, the Lord Jesus Christ who has laid down His life for His sheep to bring us peace and life itself.

SELF-ASSESSMENT

On a scale of 1 to 5, how developed are you in the competency of shepherding?

1	2	3	4	5
"I admit I am clueless in this competency."	"I know enough to know what I don't know."	"I can get by."	"I have a healthy skill set in this competency."	"I'm killing it in this area."

CHAPTER 20

PEACEMAKING

Emotionally exhausted, Tate simply wanted to walk away. As associate pastor in a growing church, Tate regularly found himself in the role of mediator between Greg (the lead pastor) and several staff members and the occasional elder, deacon, and small group leader. He knew that conflict was growing by the day, and to engage it would likely cost him friendships, the respect of colleagues, and potentially his job.

The problem intensified when Tate learned that a number of staff frequently talked about the problem with one another, thus forming relational triangles. Tate consistently worked to collapse triangles by encouraging the staff to meet with Greg one-on-one, but history showed that those meetings went poorly. In fact, three staff members in the past year found themselves looking for new jobs after a one-on-one with Greg.

Tate knew that engaging Greg would likely lead to an argument, which was recurrently a relational dead end. A champion college debater, Greg effectively employed those skills whenever confronted. The situation had grown so desperate that a number of staff threatened a mass resignation if something wasn't done soon to confront Greg and his management style, which constantly had everyone on edge. Several small group leaders had already walked away, insisting that they would rather serve in a church where they weren't intimidated by the pastor.

As a young pastor, I wish I would have understood that church conflict is inevitable. I spent so much time in my early years of ministry avoiding conflict that I unknowingly fed the conflict monster. The question is not if you will get your nose bent out of shape but when—and the extent of the adenoidal damage! As we all know, where two or three are gathered, there will be conflict. In the New Testament, we see conflict between James, John, and the rest of the disciples (Mark 10:35–41), Peter and Paul (Gal. 2:11–14), and Paul and Barnabas (Acts 15:36–39), just to name a few. Unresolved conflict can fracture trust, do damage to relationships, and weaken or, in some cases, destroy a local church.

> What is commonly defined as peace in a local church is nothing more than a cold war truce in which conflict contributors reluctantly agree to a temporary ceasefire.

When encountering conflict, we have no choice but to lean in. While it would be easier to ignore, we must work through it. Seeking to resolve conflict in a biblical manner is not optional. Peacemaking is a gospel mandate (Rom. 12:18). As a leader, you must become proficient in conflict resolution, or you will have an intensely difficult time leading in the Lord's work. Leading from a place of insincerity, where the main goal is a ceasefire rather than biblical peace, will be quickly sniffed out by the congregation. God calls His shepherds to lead transformationally, not transactionally.

Peacemaking in the Local Church

Conflict is no joy ride for anyone. Conflict can lead to increased levels of stress, a loss of sleep, and amplified anxiety. Biblical peace is not the absence of conflict but rather active faith in Jesus Christ in the midst of conflict. What is commonly defined as peace in a local church is nothing more than a cold war truce in which conflict contributors reluctantly agree to a temporary ceasefire. Biblical peace creates a Christ-centered righteousness that brings people together in love. Peace is impossible without a radical change in our human nature. The Hebrew word *shalom* carries the idea of much more than the absence of trouble. Shalom means wholeness and overall well-being. In the days of the Old Testament, for someone to bless you with the shalom of the Lord meant that they were asking the Lord to bless you with a full life.

Although conflict is unpleasant, conflict itself is never the core problem. Conflict is the check engine light on your car's dashboard that tells you to look under the hood to see what's wrong. When we encounter conflict, we must take courage and explore what lies beneath, usually dealing with fear, hurt, and insecurity. The presenting conflict is rarely if ever the real conflict.

Jesus says, "Blessed are the peacemakers, for they will be called sons of God" (Matt. 5:9). Peacemaking is always a risk. Any attempt at it carries the possibility of even more conflict. To be sure, it often seems so much easier to let things slide. However, conflict that slides only slides into a pile. It doesn't disappear.

Painting with broad brushstrokes, there are three types of conflict: internal (conflict with one's self), external (conflict with others and creation), and divine (conflict with God). While all three are important to address, this chapter focuses on external conflict we experience with fellow believers, specifically in the form of relational triangles.

Three Types of Relational Triangles

Many believe that a good Christian never gets angry. So, when they do encounter conflict, they tend to deal with it by denial. When the conflict continues, if they are unwilling to deal directly with the person with whom it concerns, they may be tempted to go tell another person. When they do this, they have formed a relational triangle, a common but immensely unhelpful way of "dealing" with conflict by multiplying it. It inevitably results in gossip, hurt feelings, and division in the church.

Collapsing relational triangles is essential to leadership in the local church. Jay Fowler, one of the Regional Executive Directors on the PastorServe team, is an expert in the area of teaching churches how to collapse relational triangles. The following wisdom is straight from Jay.

Bill and Karen have served together on their church's children's leadership team for the past three years. Bill is the full-time children's pastor, and Karen is a volunteer who serves in Sunday school about thirty times a year. Karen loves serving and is often bothered if Bill leaves her off of the schedule. One particular month, Bill fails to schedule Karen to participate in the nursery, her favorite place to serve. It was an honest mistake on Bill's part, but Karen is deeply offended, believing that Bill is intentionally sending her a passive-aggressive message that she should quit serving in the children's ministry. Bill and Karen are now in conflict.

Jesus said if we have a conflict with another person, we are to go directly to that person and talk with them about it (Matt.

18:15). The goal is to keep the conflict between just the two people so they can reconcile. In this case, if Karen would go to Bill, she would learn that the conflict was merely an oversight on Bill's part, a mistake he would readily own and immediately correct. But, instead of going to Bill, Karen chooses to go to Cindy, another volunteer member of the children's ministry team, to share her frustration with Bill. Karen has now created a relational triangle. If this sounds familiar, it's because relational triangles are the norm in many churches (and families and businesses and schools and governments and . . .).

There are three basic kinds of relational triangles.

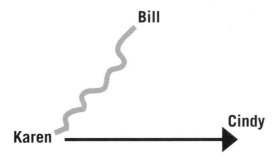

Tell-a-secret triangle

In this triangle, Karen goes to Cindy and tells her why she is angry with Bill. How could Bill be so insensitive! Doesn't he know how much serving children means to Karen? The triangle is solidified when Karen tells Cindy that she can never mention this conversation to Bill. Cindy is expected to keep Karen's secret. After unloading her secret, Karen feels a lot better. So much better that she may never have any desire to go to Bill and actually resolve the problem. The bad news is, Cindy now harbors bad feelings towards Bill. It was cruel of him to exclude Karen from the schedule. Perhaps she should quit the children's ministry team in solidarity with Karen. Cindy is now caught holding a secret and is unable to resolve her negative feelings toward Bill. She can't approach Bill without disclosing a confidential conversation, thus jeopardizing her friendship with Karen.

Send-a-message triangle

In this triangle, Karen asks Cindy to take a message to Bill. She tells Cindy to let Bill know that she didn't appreciate being left off the children's ministry schedule. "And tell Bill that I'm not surprised, because he has given hints over the past year that he doesn't want me around." (In families, you might hear, "You tell your father how mad I am at him for not picking you up after soccer practice!" In a school, it might sound like, "Tell that coach that I did not appreciate the harsh language she used when correcting my daughter during the recent volleyball game.")

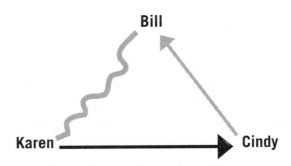

In this scenario, Karen puts Cindy in a terrible position. Try as she might, it is very difficult for Cindy to get the message exactly right. When Cindy delivers the message, Bill is caught off guard and begins to grill her about details. But Cindy can't answer the questions because she doesn't know every detail of the conflict.

She only knows what Karen has told her. Bill presses Cindy, wanting to understand why Karen feels this way and why she couldn't approach him herself.

At this point, Cindy is left with trying to make up answers or pleading ignorance. This can lead to an escalation of the conflict rather than a resolution. In the end, Cindy feels like a failure and feels the tension of being caught in the middle.

Send-a-covert-message triangle

The third kind of triangulation is similar to the second. This is when Karen wants to send a message to Bill through Cindy, but this time, Karen wants to remain hidden and anonymous. Karen asks Cindy to approach Bill and say, "I just wanted to tell you that you really offended someone on the children's ministry team. They asked me to tell you, but they did not want me to tell you their name. They just wanted you to know how hurtful and insensitive your actions have been."

Obviously, this triangle is a disaster waiting to happen. Bill is now paranoid because he doesn't know who is upset with him. He will imagine that everyone on the children's team is! Once again, Cindy feels caught in the middle, not wanting to divulge Karen as the sender of the message, but now feels bad for Bill because she understands that the offense was an honest oversight. In a worst-case scenario, Cindy can feel like she has a lot of power over Bill. Sadly, some people delight to be Cindy in this scenario. They enjoy sending messages that hurt others without having to take any personal responsibility, since, technically, the message belongs to someone else.

How to Collapse Triangles

The most important thing to remember when it comes to collapsing triangles is that Jesus told us to go to our brother or sister in private to work out our relational problems. This is because reconciliation can only happen between the two parties actually involved. When God had a problem with humanity, He showed up face-to-face in Jesus Christ to reconcile us to Himself. Since that is His way, He commands those who love and follow Him to do the same. As Paul says to the Corinthians,

> *All this is from God, who through Christ reconciled us to himself and gave us the ministry of reconciliation; that is, in Christ God was reconciling the world to himself, not counting their trespasses against them, and entrusting to us the message of reconciliation.* (2 Cor. 5:18–19)

No one can apologize on behalf of another person. No one can confess sins that another person committed. Confession, apology, showing remorse, forgiving, and reconciling are personal acts that must be done between the two parties who have hurt one another.

How to Collapse the Triangle If You Are Cindy

Suppose you are Cindy. When Karen approaches you with a problem about Bill, you should say the following:

1. "Have you had a chance to personally speak with Bill about this?" You might add, "I don't want to be in a triangle on this."

2. "Go talk with Bill as soon as possible. I will be praying for you."

3. "At the end of the week, I will check in with you to see if you had a chance to talk to Bill. If you did not, I will tell Bill that he needs to talk with you. I won't tell Bill what you said, only that there is an issue that needs to be resolved."

If Bill and Karen cannot reconcile, Cindy could offer to go with them or to find another mediator that could help them talk through their issues. This is in accordance with Matthew 18:16. If there is still a problem, Bill and Karen could ask another pastor or one of the elders of the church to help them reconcile. If the conflict is severe and the previous steps have not resolved it, churches may want to call in an outside group or ministry, like PastorServe. This is in accordance with Matthew 18:17.

How to Collapse the Triangle If You Are Karen

Suppose you are Karen, and you are the one with the grievance. Take these simple steps:

1. Speak directly to Bill. Meet face-to-face with the person who hurt you. Avoid the temptation to triangulate. There may be times when you need to process your feelings with a trusted friend like Cindy. But that is only so she can go to Bill with a clear heart and head. Hopefully, Cindy will love you enough to help you see your own sin in the situation. If you do include Cindy, it is important to report back to Cindy how the meeting unfolded, so she gets to celebrate the reconciliation, too.

2. Go humbly. Be willing to admit to Bill your part in the conflict. As Jesus says, "first take the log out of your own eye."

3. Share honestly. The Bible exhorts us to speak truthfully (Eph. 4:25). Jesus tells us we need to show our brother or sister their fault (Matt. 18:15). This should always be done respectfully and with grace (1 Peter 2:17).

4. Extend forgiveness. We have been forgiven so many sins by our Lord. We are right with God only by grace through faith in Jesus' death for us on the cross. He asks us to extend that same forgiveness to those who sin against us (Eph. 4:32).

It takes great maturity and self-control to be forthright about conflict, but it is so worth it, because it leads to trust, respect, and affection.

How to Collapse the Triangle If You Are Bill

Sometimes triangles are formed in churches because people can be dominant, prideful, unapproachable, and/or manipulative. People do not feel safe confronting this type of person. As a result, people may go to others and begin to triangulate out of frustration and fear. If you are Bill, here are some things you can do to collapse triangles:

1. Be willing to go to a person who has something against you (Matt. 5:23–24).

2. Graciously receive people who come to you with a complaint or to work through conflict.

3. Find your security in Christ's grace for you. It is hard to hear criticism. But it is easier when we can freely acknowledge our own failings and sins and know that God forgives us.

4. Listen carefully to what is shared (James 1:19).

5. Repeat back what you hear the person saying to you. Sometimes that's all people need. They may not want you to change anything. They long to be acknowledged and know they were heard.

6. Find points of agreement between you. You may not agree on everything, but start with where you do agree and focus there.

7. Be willing to admit your fault and ask for forgiveness (James 5:16).

8. Humble yourself and be willing to learn (Prov. 12:1). God may be trying to teach you something about yourself or your ministry.

9. Envision a preferred future together. In this case, how do Bill and Karen want to go forward together? What can they agree to do in the future so they will not hurt one another? True repentance always leads to changes in how we live (Matt. 3:8).

God's heart is that we be at peace with one another (Rom. 12:18). But He also knows that conflict is inevitable, even in His family. He asks us to do with one another what He modeled for us when He came in the person of Jesus Christ. No triangles. No secrets. No covert messages. He came to meet us, challenge us, and save us. He came so we could be forgiven and reconciled. That is

His heart for His family. That is what He wants us to do with each other.

Characteristics of a Peacemaker

Maybe the Karen-Bill scenario is triggering your own experiences with church conflict. Despite how it seems, you *can* promote a spirit of peace in your church. I encourage you to commit to live out the above peacemaking practices and the below peacemaking characteristics.

1. Committed

Guard the peace and purity of your church. When in conflict yourself, give others the benefit of the doubt, then go resolve it immediately. If you hear a negative report about someone, do everything you can to collapse the triangle. Additionally, when hearing a negative report, remember that there are always at minimum two sides of every story (Prov. 18:13–17).

2. Honest

A peacemaker admits failures in relationships, freely confessing that he or she is at odds with others. Peace occurs when truth is known, brokenness is acknowledged, issues are brought into the open, and parties reconcile. Peace never evades the issue. Although we all desire to avoid strife, if we sacrifice the truth, there is no real peace.

3. Forgiving

A peacemaker understands the power of forgiveness. For one, they know the power of forgiveness in their own lives, and they extend it to others. They embody Ephesians 4:32: "Be kind to one another, tenderhearted, forgiving one another as God in Christ forgave you." But second, they know that some wrongs can ultimately only be righted through forgiveness—there are no do-overs. Rather than drink the bitter poison of a grudge, they swallow the medicine of forgiveness.[30]

4. Active

Sometimes, a peacemaker stirs up trouble to bring about peace—what the late senator John Lewis called "good trouble." He or she wages peace. They understand that time does not heal all wounds. A peacemaker actively pursues peace in all of its fullness, encouraging well-being and wholeness. Jesus Christ is the Prince of Peace, and yet He created conflict (Luke 23:5). Paul the apostle caused riots nearly everywhere he traveled. And yet it was Paul who wrote, "Maintain the unity of the Spirit in the bond of peace" (Eph. 4:3), "Let us pursue what makes for peace and for mutual upbuilding" (Rom. 14:19), and "If possible, so far as it depends on you, live peaceably with all" (Rom. 12:18).

Remember that the greatest conflict in history, the conflict between God and man, was mediated by Jesus Christ through death.

5. Ready to risk pain

It can be expensive to make peace. It requires humility. It requires your heart. It can even require your tears. The peacemaker is not content with status quo as long as there is no peace. There is nothing cheap about the peacemaking of Jesus, who gave His very life to accomplish ultimate peace (Col. 1:19–20; Eph. 2:13–17).

Be a peacemaker in your church. Commit to collapsing triangles. When necessary, wage peace. Remember that the greatest conflict in history, the conflict between God and man, was mediated by Jesus Christ through death. The greatest conflict you will ever know has been resolved and vanquished at a great price, the shed blood of Jesus Christ.

SELF-ASSESSMENT

On a scale of 1 to 5, how developed are you in the competency of peacemaking?

1	2	3	4	5
"I admit I am clueless in this competency."	"I know enough to know what I don't know."	"I can get by."	"I have a healthy skill set in this competency."	"I'm killing it in this area."

PART V DISCUSSION QUESTIONS

1. On a scale of one to five (five being mastery), how developed are you in the core competency of serving the body of believers?

2. Of the sub-competencies (building biblical community, disciple-making, shepherding, peacemaking), which is your strongest? Which is your weakest?

3. What is one way you can lean into your strongest sub-competencies?

4. What is a practice you can implement this week to grow in your weakest sub-competencies?

5. Who could you partner with to cover your weaknesses and minister more effectively together?

PART VI

Grow the Body of Believers

CHAPTER 21

THEOLOGY OF MISSIONS

I have traveled to the nation of Haiti more than fifty times to serve the country's leaders. Once you travel that many times to a particular country, right or wrong, people consider you an expert on it. I am regularly asked, "What is your vision for Haiti? How can Haiti be fixed?" Perhaps you know where this is going.

I do not have a vision for how to "fix" Haiti. I have not constructed a Haiti recovery plan. It is not my job to have a vision for Haiti. It is the job of Haitian leaders to have a vision for Haiti; it is my job to identify godly Haitian leaders and do everything in my power to support their vision for Haiti. I'll take this a step further. It is offensive and arrogant to think that as an American, I would have a vision for a country other than my own. Recently, I led a team of highly competent business leaders on a trip to Haiti. An East coast CEO of a multibillion-dollar corporation, before he had even been in country for five hours, began explaining to anyone who would listen how to fix the ills of the impoverished nation. And why not? After all, Americans can fix anything, right? While I trust that he was sincerely trying to help, I found his ignorance and arrogance particularly offensive.

It is not the job of the American church to fix the world. That said, I love exposing US leaders to the needs of developing countries, and I do believe the material wealth of America can radically impact the world if we catch a vision for kingdom-of-God returns on investment. In fact, one of my callings is to facilitate this connection. But it goes far beyond material support. I believe that it is vital for leaders within the local church to understand our missional calling to the nations, our need to know the nations, and the wisdom of focusing on just a few nations.

Calling to the Nations:
Every Believer's Mission

When people inform me that they are praying for revival, I remind them to keep praying *and rejoice*, because their prayers are being radically answered! The church is growing at an extraordinary rate. The gospel is bringing radical change and shedding the light of Christ in the darkest of corners. When people respond with skepticism, I remind them that the church is experiencing growth as never before, nearly everywhere *except* in the West. In Latin America, South America, Africa, Asia, and beyond, the growth of the local church is unprecedented. This naturally begs the question, why is the developed world spiritually declining while the developing world experiences revival?

The Western church is in steep decline chiefly because it has neglected God's primary mission of being worshiped by all people groups on earth (Rom. 15:20–21). Many in the Western church fail to understand that God is a missional God (Gen. 12:1–4a; Matt. 28:18–20). We have abdicated the mandate and the example of the Lord Jesus that believers are called to be a light to all nations (Isa. 49:6–8; 2 Cor. 4:6). The Western church has often neglected the Lord's call to minister to the totality of human need (Matt. 22:37–39; 25:31–46). We have understood God's call to the nations as an optional program instead of a core element of every local church. We have unsuccessfully attempted to align God's cross-cultural, kingdom-advancing mandate to our self-serving agenda. We have embraced God's missional call, as long as it doesn't infringe on our advantaged lifestyle. We have simultaneously insulated and isolated ourselves from both the needs of the world and God's global activity.

Simply stated, the Western church is commonly infatuated with the trappings of wealth, influence, safety, and comfort. These idols have made God's calling to the nations a secondary priority, draining God's call to the nations of any urgency. Let me tell you a story that stands in stark contrast.

Witnessed truth is the most powerful form of education. Many years ago, I was privileged to co-lead a team ministering in China. On one particular night, our team met at 10:00 p.m. for a late-night "educational" excursion. Several of us piled into a van and traversed the city streets for ninety minutes. When our "guide" was convinced we were not being followed, he instructed us to duck our heads. Peering out the window, I could see that we had turned down a darkened street. We slowly proceeded towards what appeared to be a dead end. Suddenly, two large planters moved to the sides, exposing a garage. The door was quickly raised, we pulled the van into the garage, the door went down, and the planters were returned to their place. While it felt like a scene from a James Bond movie, this was real, and everyone understood what was at stake. Our guide asked us to stay perfectly still and make no sound. After a couple of minutes, we quietly opened the van door and proceeded into the adjoining three-story structure.

Every window was covered in a permanent black shade. From the street, the building looked like an uninhabited structure. Inside it was a thriving underground Chinese seminary. We walked in silence from room to room, each with several bunk-style beds and the students' belongings neatly laid out: a Bible, several books, and one change of clothes.

Now midnight, we were escorted into a large room where we encountered approximately forty young Chinese believers. Speaking in hushed tones, we were informed that each student was between the ages of eighteen and twenty-four. Each had made a three-year commitment to live in the seminary, agreeing to stay inside the structure. Each month, one or two students were allowed to leave to purchase groceries and supplies, which meant that a student might venture outside once in a calendar year. They were there because their local church believed that God had uniquely gifted them to carry the gospel to the ends of the earth.

Sitting in the room with young radical believers who had surrendered all for Jesus was incredibly humbling. Our host asked me and another pastor to say a word of encouragement to the students. A wave of inadequacy swept over me. What right did I have to address these disciples of Jesus? As I stood before the group, I whispered, "I have nothing to say to you other than to thank you. Thank you for surrendering everything to Jesus." The host translated, which gave me a moment to compose my thoughts. I went on to affirm that the struggle to which they had given their lives was a worthy cause. I remember thinking that I needed one of these students to come to the United States in order to help the American church understand mission, persecution, sacrifice, and unyielding commitment to Jesus.

After another American pastor spoke to the students, we

continued to walk through the structure. As we passed through one particular classroom, we noticed maps on every wall. One map had arrows pointing from the location of the seminary to every corner of China. Another detailed the plan to reach the Middle East. Finally, and most sobering, a map showed arrows coming from China to the United States. The majority of the arrows pointed to Southern California. Beneath the arrows was written in English, "Goal: Reach Los Angeles for Jesus."

These young Chinese seminary students understood God's missional calling to reach the nations. They grasped that the mandate from the God of the universe is to take the gospel to all nations. Their lives demonstrated their understanding that the God of the Bible is a missional God. And one primary focus of their prayers was to reach the United States, starting with L.A. I have shared this with a number of American believers who were deeply offended. Why? Because our arrogance and America-first mindset has convinced us that America is always necessarily the giver and never the recipient. That mindset all too commonly extends into the local church. America sends missionaries to the world, not the other way around! Americans believers need to accept the fact that many nations rightly view America as a mission field to be reached, and they are actively sending teams to reach what they rightly perceive to be one of the more ungodly nations. One night in a secret Chinese seminary made that clear.

Knowledge of the Nations: Growing in Global Understanding

If we are called to reach the world, it stands to reason we should know the world's needs. As a leader, are you in touch with those? At any one time, there are several dozen wars raging around the world. Can you name ten of them? Five? One? Or, bringing this to a very practical level, are you in touch with the needs of your local community? It is not for lack of information that we do not know; it is because we do not ask.

Though you may be geographically isolated from the needs of the world, do not be geographically insulated. Ask questions! Get in touch with the needs of the world and pass the information along to those under your leadership. When you encounter people with global experiences, ask them, "Would you share your story of growing up in South Africa?" or, "As one engaged with the Muslim population, can you help me understand the best way to meet their needs?"

How aware is your local church that there are presently more than 140 million orphans around the world? Does your church have any understanding that in Africa, 95.3% of those who die are passing away without any medical treatment? In Latin America, the number is 99.4%. Have you helped to educate your church that there are around 1 billion people living at the margins of survival on less than one US dollar a day, with 2.6 billion—40 percent of world—living on less than two? How does your church respond to the fact that 982 million people across the world are hungry? One of the jobs of the pastor is to expose the church to need.

An evangelist who regularly travels to the nations once told me that while John 3:16 was far and away the most popular Bible verse in America, Matthew 5:10–12 was the most beloved around the world. The passage reads,

"Blessed are those who are persecuted for righteousness' sake, for theirs is the kingdom of heaven.

"Blessed are you when others revile you and persecute you and utter all kinds of evil against you falsely on my account. Rejoice and be glad, for your reward is great in heaven, for so they persecuted the prophets who were before you."

As believers, we must accept what is widely understood throughout the world, that following Jesus will involve hardship, sacrifice, persecution, suffering, and, in some cases, even death.

In the US, we have generally marginalized biblical teaching that clearly defines the consequences of following the Lord Jesus. Throughout His life, Jesus spelled out the suffering that would inevitably visit every disciple. Likewise, Paul demonstrated the hardships and afflictions of following Jesus, including beatings and imprisonment (2 Cor. 1:4; 4:8–9, 17–18; Phil. 1:29). Second Timothy 3:12 tells us in the plainest language, "Indeed, all who desire to live a godly life in Christ Jesus will be persecuted."

As a leader, take time to educate those under your care regarding the persecuted church around the world. Specifically, lead in praying for believers in China, North Korea, Somalia, Afghanistan, Pakistan, Sudan, Syria, Saudi Arabia, Iran, Iraq, Yemen, and other countries where followers of Jesus regularly encounter intense persecution. Talk about the need to pray for our brothers and sisters in Christ who live under ever-increasing Islamic radicalization in sub-Saharan Africa. Remind your church that your body is part of the greater family of God, and that nearly one in every twelve members in your family live in a culture or place where Christianity is illegal or punished.[31]

It's a simple law of physics: forward motion necessarily involves friction. If you are in the will of God, there will be opposition. Doing the work of the Lord will result in pain and suffering, possibly death. It is possible to be outside of the will of God and living a seemly successful life, while it is equally possible to be right in the middle of God's will and endure great suffering. When, after a lifetime of deception, Jacob finally yielded to God's will, the Lord literally beat him up (Gen. 32:22–32). When Joseph maintained his moral purity, his reward was prison (Gen. 39). Following the feeding of the five thousand, Jesus sends the disciples into a storm (Matt. 14:22–24). If the disciples had *disobeyed* Jesus, they could have been sitting around a warm fire, eating a good meal while swapping stories about the day. Instead, obedience led them into a storm. Jesus was living a perfect life when He was crucified on a cross. When you walk by faith, you will encounter opposition from those who walk by sight. Sadly, I have found that a theology of suffering is seldom present in the American church. I encourage you to reread chapter 4 of this book, Renaut's incredible insights into God's call to suffer.

Focusing on a Few Nations: Putting Down Deep Roots

As a twenty-five-year-old, I was a walking definition of arrogance and pride. One area that fed my egotism was that I was well on my way to visiting every country in the world. With parents who loved to travel and a brother whose family served as missionaries in France, I had already traveled to nearly sixty countries around the world. In my self-centeredness, the number one item on my bucket list was to visit every country in the world.

It was at that point in life, serving at Grace Chapel in Lexington, Massachusetts, under missions pastor Paul Borthwick, that the Lord "revised" my perspective on the world. I realized that my self-worth and passport stamps were intimately connected. I began to understand that the "impact" I was making on the world was about an inch deep, if that. Under the conviction of the Holy Spirit, I committed to taking several years to explore the Lord's calling on my life regarding the nations. Over the next decade, the Lord made very clear that my focus would be Haiti, Trinidad, China, and Israel. If you look at my last four passports, you will see that my travel has been almost exclusively to those four countries. I want to be used of the Lord to make a significant impact in each of these countries, and that can only happen as you go deep in select locations.

Pastoring a local body of believers, I brought that same mindset into our church. Rather than encourage traveling to different locations every year, we selected areas around the world to concentrate our efforts. We committed to working with local churches and ministries in just three countries. At one location in France, we sent a team of a dozen of our church's best leaders to serve for one year. It was a substantial investment of time, finances, and resources. The satisfaction our church found in knowing that we had moved the needle for the kingdom in one particular region of France was incredible.

Few would argue that the United States has experienced blessings far beyond what we deserve. Do you ever ask yourself why? Psalm 67:1–2 answers that question:

> *May God be gracious to us and bless us*
> *and make his face to shine upon us. . . .*
> *That your way may be known on earth,*
> *your saving power among all nations.*

The Lord has extended unfathomable grace, mercy, and blessings to us. Why? So that we would take His gospel to the nations.

SELF-ASSESSMENT

On a scale of 1 to 5, how developed are you in the competency of theology of missions?

1	2	3	4	5
"I admit I am clueless in this competency."	"I know enough to know what I don't know."	"I can get by."	"I have a healthy skill set in this competency."	"I'm killing it in this area."

CHAPTER 22

REPRODUCING AND REVITALIZING THE LOCAL CHURCH

Life is filled with numerous stories of what might have been. What might have been if I had taken a different job, if I had attended a different school, if I had married a different woman? What might have been if I had invested $5,000 in Apple on December 12, 1980, the date of Apple's IPO? (You would be a *multi*millionaire.) What might have been if I would have played the lottery the night they chose my lucky numbers? (If you followed the standard lottery winner's story, you would be friendless, miserable, broke, and likely divorced.)

One of my favorite What Might Have Been stories revolves around Woodstock, the music festival that over four days in August 1969 changed the course of music history. Some of the greatest musical artists trace their rise to the avalanche of publicity that came as a result of performing there. Held at Max Yasgur's farm in the New York Catskills, Woodstock artists included Joan Baez, Santana, the Grateful Dead, Janis Joplin, The Who, Creedence Clearwater Revival, Jefferson Airplane, Sly and the Family Stone,

Jimi Hendrix, and many, many others. More interesting than that list is the list of artists who were invited but declined because, after all, who wants to play at a pig farm in Bethel, New York?

The Byrds were invited but chose not to participate, figuring Woodstock would be no different than any other of the countless music festivals held that summer. Tommy James stated later, "We could have just kicked ourselves. . . . we realized what we'd missed a couple of days later."[32] Mind Garage and Spirit both declined because they had higher-paying gigs elsewhere. Joni Mitchell was slated to perform but canceled when her manager urged her to take a much higher-profile appearance on the *The Dick Cavett Show*. While Joni Mitchell, the Byrds, and Tommy James did go on to make names for themselves, I am guessing that Mind Garage and Spirit regularly kicked themselves as they faded into relative obscurity.

I know of numerous pastors and churches around the country that all too often engage in the fruitless mind game of What Might Have Been. What if I had planted a church rather than working to revitalize an established church? (In other words, is it true what they say about it being easier to give birth than it is to raise the dead?) What if I had worked at church health and facilitated church growth, not the other way around? What if I had done everything in my power to first and foremost nurture spiritual maturity? What if my ambition had been to skillfully shepherd the flock that God entrusted to me rather than tirelessly working to have more than God intended? What if I had led my church to plant numerous small congregations rather than go to questionable lengths to grow a megachurch? These what-ifs could go on *ad infinitum*. The point is: an obsession with What Might Have Been is ultimately an assault on the sovereignty of God. Stop wishing you would have placed yourself in a healthier situation. Don't find yourself looking through the rearview mirror. Begin working to bring health and vitality to the church where you serve—now.

Church Health over Church Growth

The majority of churches in the US are either stagnant or declining. While the actual percentage of declining churches is debated (estimates range from 60 to 84 percent), no one is debating that the American church is largely in decline. In fact, even conversion percentages in new churches have steadily declined. Whereas church plants historically had three to four times the conversation rate per attendee than established churches, those numbers have significantly dropped. We can no longer plant and grow new churches fast enough to outrun the increase in population coupled with the decline of existing churches. We are reaping the destructive seeds of compromise that were sown during the church growth movement, when growth at any cost was center stage and church health was left standing in the wings. The result is a largely petrified church in desperate need of revitalization.

Pursuing church growth as the primary objective will ultimately lead to the demise of the local church. Pursuing grace-centered health as the initial objective breathes life into the local church. Church growth and reproduction are the fruit, not the root, of a vibrant, healthy church. We should celebrate this. But church growth built on compromise? We should mourn it. There are many outstanding megachurches that have faithfully preached the gospel—their goal—and experienced significant growth—the result. The two should not be confused.

That said, big does not automatically mean unhealthy. Over

four decades of ministry, I have occasionally connected with those who are skeptical of anything that resembles church growth. This scarcity mindset equates church growth with biblical compromise. They are looking for a narrative to justify their lifeless congregation, drawing a target around their dart that landed far from the bullseye.

Far too many congregations have relied on church growth methodology rather than the Holy Spirit. Os Guinness suggests we would be wise to remember Origen's guidance: "Christians are free to plunder the Egyptians but forbidden to set up a golden calf."[33] He builds on this principle when he writes, "By all means plunder freely of the treasures of modernity, but in God's name make sure that what comes out of the fire, which will test our life's endeavors, is gold fit for the temple of God and not ... [the] image of a golden calf."[34] In the remainder of this chapter, I will outline seven marks of healthy, thriving, reproducing churches.

Seven Marks of Thriving Churches

Whether you are in the early days of a church plant or you are seeking to revitalize a congregation, the following characteristics are essential to understanding how the Lord builds His church.

1. Thriving congregations are the work of the Holy Spirit

Before my wife and I launched a church in Kansas City, I made a pilgrimage to sit at the feet of Tim Kirk, a respected Indianapolis church planter. I asked Tim what he had learned about church growth that would be applicable to our plant. His answer still resonates today. Tim took a deep breath and said, "Jimmy, the Lord will build His church" (see Matt. 16:18). I assured Tim that I was well aware that the Lord alone would build His church, but I needed some practical advice for how to (quickly) build my church. Tim repeated, "The Lord will build His church." I was getting frustrated. I needed practical advice for building a thriving local body of believers. I assured Tim that I agreed with his assessment. I 100 percent understood his point, which was well taken, but—Tim interrupted me, "Jimmy, I know you say you understand, but you will not fully understand until you plant the church."

I didn't understand what Tim meant until we were a year into the church plant. I couldn't have been more frustrated with the fluctuation in worship attendance. I was dumbfounded by the reasons people left and continually surprised by the reasons people gave for coming. Tim's words echoed through my mind, and I believed them. Years later, when the church had experienced growth and we had planted our first daughter church, a young church planter approached me to ask about the "secret" to growing a church. You can guess my response.

> There is no formula guaranteeing numerical success. There is a "formula" for church health, though: utter reliance upon the Holy Spirit, evidenced by the centrality of prayer and the faithful preaching of the gospel.

At PastorServe, we regularly consult with churches we would sadly describe as a mile wide and a fraction of an inch deep. The emphasis is squarely on the frontstage perception rather than backstage character. Personally, I understand how churches have come to the place of a formulaic approach to growth. I remember attending a church planting conference in the early '90s where the emphasis was solely upon planting and growing a large church. Church health was nowhere to be found at the seminar. As young, aspiring, impressionable church planters, we were taught a simple formula to launch a church that exceeded the most challenging growth barrier of one hundred on day one (30,000 contacts × .10 × .10 ÷ 2 = 150+). No doubt, many leaders bought into this same strategy. While by God's grace we did emphasize gospel health, it was not our primary pursuit. Growing a large church was job one.

The truth is, there is no formula guaranteeing numerical success. There is a "formula" for church health, though: utter reliance upon the Holy Spirit, evidenced by the centrality of prayer and the faithful preaching of the gospel. The Lord builds His church.

2. Thriving congregations *work* at church health and *facilitate* church growth

I have had the privilege of traveling to developing countries on more than 130 occasions to partner with local churches and ministries. I have preached in cathedrals in Europe and have delivered the Word in dilapidated buildings in Africa, Asia, South America, and throughout the Caribbean. I've seen worship teams play music on instruments that would be discarded as trash in America. I have been interrupted during sermons by countless animals, including jumping goats and flying chickens. I have preached in Haiti when the power kept going out during a nighttime worship service, more times than I could count. And my favorite, I have experienced little orphans wrapping themselves around my leg as I preached. I have witnessed very few churches in developing countries produce a worship service that I would label a performance designed to grow the church.

God calls you to feed your church, not to grow it.

As such, your job is to work at church health. I am grateful for the work of Steve Macchia and the team at Leadership Transformations. In his excellent book *Becoming a Healthy Church*, Steve presents his research from interviewing more than two thousand churches and church leaders. Steve writes that at its foundation, "a healthy church is prayerful in all of the following aspects of church life and ministry, is reliant upon God's power and the authority of his Word, and values:

1. God's Empowering Presence

2. God-Exalting Worship

3. Spiritual Disciplines

4. Learning and Growing in Community

5. A Commitment to Loving, Caring Relationships

6. Servant-Leadership Development

7. An Outward Focus: evangelism, social concern, and international missions

8. Wise Administration and Accountability

9. Networking with the Body of Christ

10. Stewardship and Generosity"[35]

Look over the list again. Nowhere does Steve define numerical growth as a mark of a healthy church. However, a healthy church will more often than not experience numerical growth.

3. Thriving congregations center around the person of Jesus Christ

Anthropocentrism is the belief that human beings, not God, are the center of the universe. This perspective fails to acknowledge that we are called to worship before an audience of one. Søren Kierkegaard famously wrote that we tend to think of church as a kind of theater. We (the congregation) sit in the audience, attentively watching the actors (the choir or worship team) onstage. If satisfactorily entertained, we express gratitude with applause. Church, Kierkegaard argued, should be the opposite of theater. We (the congregation) are the "performers," God the audience. Therefore, we should leave a worship service asking ourselves not, "What did I get out of that service?" but rather "Was God pleased with our worship?"

When mankind is the focus, pragmatism trumps principles. Relevance and contextualization become the axioms of the day. Theology takes a back seat to methodology and superficiality becomes the norm. When methodology takes the lead, it goes in search of a theology to support it.

Like any pastor, I have experienced weekends where everything was in perfect sync. The worship, the message, and the audience all combined to create "the perfect worship service." And I have walked away from many of those weekends feeling empty, believing that few lives if any were changed. Conversely, I have had weekends where everything fell apart. The music was disjointed, the PowerPoint was three slides behind, the message was poorly delivered, and (you know where this is going) a young family approaches in tears saying they have never been so moved by the Holy Spirit during a worship service and will be making this their church home.

During the early years of the Kansas City church plant, we ordained a young staff member named Scott Sauls, whom God has since used to minister to many through his preaching, writing, and leadership. His ordination message was delivered by Dr. Dan Doriani, a professor at Covenant Theological Seminary. I will never forget Dan's words to Scott: "Scott, this is not the seminary classroom. A message that may have received an A grade at Covenant may reach no one, while a message that may have received a C may reach the masses. Don't preach sermons designed to receive an A. Preach messages that speak to the heart." Wise counsel, indeed.

4. Thriving congregations commit to birthing new churches

Church planting creates opportunity. New churches commonly mean newer, younger, and often innovative leaders and ideas. New churches create new research, new models, and new ideas for existing churches. I remember Tim Keller telling a large group of business leaders to actively support church planting in their community because in many ways, church plants are the research and development division of the church.

> Commit to kingdom collaboration, remembering that it takes all types of churches to reach all types of people.

Every congregation should prioritize church planting. Indeed, to keep pace with population growth, leaders must commit to both revitalization and church planting. Both are essential to reach our communities. If your church doesn't possess the funding to launch a daughter church, partner with another local church. Some of the best church planting stories happen when churches from differing denominations or networks join together to plant a church. Commit to kingdom collaboration, remembering that it takes all types of churches to reach all types of people.

5. Thriving congregations are both spiritually and organizationally healthy

A thriving church cannot be identified by weekly attendance, size of the budget, or even community impact. Sadly, there are many high-profile churches significantly impacting their local community while the church itself remains fundamentally unhealthy. Far too many churches tolerate spiritual and organizational dysfunction in exchange for growth and influence. Spiritual abuse can hide beneath an impressive exterior. Large churches are just as likely as small ones to struggle with politics, spiritual immaturity, infighting, competing strategies, and other common organizational struggles. A truly thriving church is more focused on spiritual and organizational health than on numerical growth.

Additionally, healthy churches respond to shifting demographics, social change, and economic challenges with relative ease. The COVID-19 pandemic of 2020 necessitated that churches quickly adjust to a rapidly changing cultural landscape. Overnight, churches that were organizationally healthy met the challenge with unprecedented innovation.

6. Thriving churches have a clearly defined vision and mission

Thriving churches have a clear picture of where they are going. They are not expending energy chasing the latest and greatest program in a vain attempt to find the church growth golden egg.

I remember doing an assessment of a church that had been experiencing struggles and was looking for help overcoming stagnation. They longed for revitalization and looked to PastorServe to provide insight. Our first agenda item was to walk through the facility. I quickly noted banners in the hallways announcing a new spiritual development program. While I hadn't heard of the program, at first glance it looked to have substance and match the church goals for spiritual development. As I ventured into the next hallway, I encountered another set of signs publicizing a different spiritual development program. I made a mental note to ask about this at the conclusion of our tour. By the time we had finished, we had seen materials for five different spiritual growth programs. When I inquired what was going on, the pastor sheepishly admitted to chasing every program that could potentially breathe life into his church.

As we discussed in chapter 9, you must define your ultimate goal (vision), daily focus (mission), and values (philosophy of ministry). For example, ours at PastorServe are:

Vision: No pastor walks alone.
Mission: Strengthen the church by serving pastors.
Values: Care, the gospel, authenticity and integrity, confidentiality, the value of the local church, collaboration, and leading catalytic movements.

Core values will differ from church to church. The key is to be selective. Don't chase after every new program that promises increased attendance. Look for a program that encourages spiritual growth over numerical growth and that feels true to your church and community.

7. Thriving churches are led by healthy pastors

It is said that pastors are hired for their frontstage ability but fired for their backstage chaos. The frontstage is what a pastor does, while the backstage is who a pastor is. A thriving pastor knows that both are important, but in the long run, who they are backstage matters much more. Thriving pastors give more attention to their backstage life than their frontstage concerns. They maintain spiritual integrity and prioritize spiritual disciplines. They are Spirit-filled leaders striving to be servants, not celebrities. Rather than be the hero, they recruit, train, and develop a team to lead and govern their congregation in pursuit of a God-given mission and vision.

It is refreshing to witness the return to church health as the primary objective in the local church. As we leave the church growth movement and enter the church health movement, the kingdom of God is the beneficiary, as the church looks to the heart rather than the head count.

SELF-ASSESSMENT

On a scale of 1 to 5, how developed are you in the competency of reproducing and revitalizing the local church?

1	2	3	4	5
"I admit I am clueless in this competency."	"I know enough to know what I don't know."	"I can get by."	"I have a healthy skill set in this competency."	"I'm killing it in this area."

CHAPTER 23

MERCY AND JUSTICE

Though we remember Moses as delivering ten laws to the Israelites (the Ten Commandments), he actually delivered 613. David condensed them to fifteen, Isaiah to eleven, and Micah to three. Later, Jesus would summarize all the law and the prophets in just two: love God and love your neighbor.

Like many, I am drawn to the way Micah 6:8 phrases our duties before God:

> *He has told you, O man, what is good;*
>   *and what does the LORD require of you*
> *but to do justice, and to love kindness,*
>   *and to walk humbly with your God?*

But what does it mean to do justice, love kindness (mercy), and walk humbly with God? While many in our culture speak of the need for justice and mercy, few comprehend their true nature.

In this life, mercy means caring for others from gospel-fueled compassion. Justice means speaking up for those whose voices have been stolen. Justice is laboring for what is fair, what is right, what brings peace, and what visibly demonstrates respect for all people as image bearers of God. It is advocating for those with less social power and financial means. Tim Keller, founding pastor of Redeemer Presbyterian Church in New York, writes that "a gospel-preaching church should be famous for its mercy and justice, or outsiders will not listen to what is being preached."[36]

I am thankful that this book will be available in English, Spanish, and Portuguese. I am aware that many readers do not reside in the US. While many of the issues raised in this chapter are pertinent to the US, everyone faces issues of mercy and justice wherever they live. I encourage readers to find the issues of injustice, oppression, and racism in their communities, and to speak truth and take action for righteousness' sake.

Systemic Racism

If you are a white American, you need to come to grips with the following reality. We live in a nation gripped by systemic racism, implicit bias, and injustice. You may have no idea what that means or how that impacts you daily. The majority of white evangelicals live in a sheltered world where they have convinced themselves that Barack Obama, Michael Jordan, and Oprah Winfrey are but a few examples of the American dream that is available to all, regardless of race, gender, or religion. This is simply untrue.

Systemic racism (also known as institutional racism) is the most dangerous form of racism alive today. It has precariously worked its way into every corner of culture, and we are largely unaware. Systemic racism is dangerous in part because it is difficult to detect—it is not as obvious as a lynching or separate water fountains, so many simply don't believe it exists. While we may be able to accurately identify and condemn examples of blatant prejudice, hate crimes, white supremacy, and anti-immigration rhetoric, systemic racism is more about education, employment, wealth, health care, housing, and general opportunity. Systemic racism is an often-undistinguishable way of thinking that can be found in schools, office buildings, hospital emergency rooms, police departments, courtrooms, prison yards, and crosswalks.

Centuries of racial injustice, which has seeped into every crack of the societal strata, cannot be removed overnight. Confronting injustice takes the full body of believers (and all people) standing shoulder to shoulder, hand in hand to effectively confront the evil before us. Systemic racism is deeply intertwined within refugee and immigration issues, high-interest payday loans, homelessness, the need for tutoring (particularly in the area of reading), the need for immigrants to learn English, and the lack of healthy food options in the urban core.

Systemic racism begins early in life when black students find themselves suspended three times more than their white peers for the same infractions. Systemic racism is about life-altering decisions made every day by people who would never consider themselves racist. It is about names like Alonzo Smith, Ahmaud Arbery, and George Floyd—names often forgotten, ignored, or unknown in the white community but revered and remembered in the black community. Systemic racism is revealed when job applicants with white-sounding names get called back twice as often as applicants with black-sounding names, even when they have identical résumés.

Whereas Jews, mainline Protestants, and Unitarians played a role in the civil rights movement, white evangelical involvement was the exception rather than the norm. Repeating the past, evangelicals today have largely abdicated our responsibility to live as one holy spiritual body. Too often, when one part of the body suffers, another part of the body turns away. As a leader, you must have a blazing hot passion for justice and mercy (Ps. 119:53). And yet, all too often, when it comes to institutional racism, white evangelicals are at best woefully naïve, often silently complicit, and sometimes even actively supportive.

I know of no white evangelical more passionate for racial equality than my son Mark. I have seen Mark shed many tears as he watched the oppression of people who did not have the opportunities afforded to him because he is a white male born in the United States. Mark, a pastor, regularly communicates that every human system (government, education, health care, criminal justice, etc.) throughout all of history has a built-in propensity to favor one group over another. Because of sin, there is no perfect system. Every human institution is going to fall one way or another. But as Mark reminds us, the glaring exception is the church of Jesus Christ.

The church is God's chosen institution to usher in the kingdom of our Lord Jesus Christ. The church is not only the mouthpiece of the gospel, it is the main vehicle through which God administers justice and offers peace. The church is God's agent for caring for the poor, the widow, the orphan, and the oppressed. That is why it is particularly shameful and egregious when the church has participated in and perpetuated the very oppression that we are called to fight against. The American church must reckon with our complicity or active involvement in the oppression of all minorities. If we turn a blind eye to this, I fear that our witness will become ineffective.

The Muddy Waters of Injustice

I remember an African American friend asking me if I had sat my children down and had the "receipt talk" with them. With a blank look in my eyes, I told him I had no idea what he was talking about. He went on to tell me that every African American parent has the receipt talk with their children. They are taught that no matter what you purchase in a store, no matter how small the purchase, you always ask for a receipt. Even for a quarter lollipop. That way, if you are accused of stealing the merchandise, you can prove that it was legitimately purchased. I had no idea.

He went on to inform me about the "when you are pulled over by the police" talk. According to one report,[37] blacks are 20% more likely to be pulled over by police than whites. Shockingly, blacks are 50% more likely to die crossing the street than whites, because drivers are less likely to stop for blacks in a crosswalk.[38] Another study revealed that black youth are two times more likely to be unemployed than white youth, two times more likely to live below the poverty line, seven times more likely to be incarcerated (black males between eighteen and nineteen), and seventeen times more likely to die from gun violence than whites. The statistics are eerily similar for Hispanics—42.8% of Hispanic youth say they fear gun violence, compared with 15.6% of white youth.[39]

As a leader of God's people, we are called to boldly stand for the oppressed. We must be willing to walk into the muddy waters of injustice. We must ask God for the courage to stand against overt racism, systemic racism, and ecclesiastical racism. I encourage you to read books that will open your eyes to the underlying ills that infect our culture. I was profoundly impacted by *Dear White Christian: What Every White Christian Needs to Know*

About How Black Christians See, Think, and Experience Racism in America (Aaron Layton) and *White Awake: An Honest Look at What It Means to Be White* (Daniel Hill). Diving into a world that will leave you uncomfortable may be the very best thing for you. Serving the oppressed, the orphan, the widow, and the immigrant are among the purest expressions of the gospel (James 1:27).

Stepping into a Hard Journey

I'll never forget the first time I saw my father cry.

The year was 1976. As a family, we had followed the Lord's leading to increase our involvement in our community of Wichita, Kansas. We believed the Lord was calling us to step into the world of foster care. And, as anyone who has ever ventured into that world will tell you, we had no idea what we were getting ourselves into.

Like many mercy ministries in the church, foster care is messy. If you are looking for easy, clean, predictable areas in which to serve, look elsewhere. In many cases, foster care will challenge the strongest of families. And in most cases, it will break your heart. Foster care can and often does turn your world upside down, challenging you emotionally, spiritually, and financially. And yet, foster care will teach lessons of grace, love, acceptance, and mercy that will transform your family. Foster care will open your eyes to a better understanding of what the Lord has done to welcome you into His forever family.

Emily was a fourteen-year-old child with the rap sheet of a forty-year-old career criminal. A ward of the state of Kansas, Emily was trapped in the dark recesses of the labyrinth that is the foster care system. She had never lasted for more than twelve weeks in any one home. Her life had been spent bouncing between juvenile detention and families who were initially determined to love

Emily and soon found the challenge to be overwhelming. Emily was a thief, a drug addict, a gang member, and a proficient liar. Emily had her first abortion at the age of thirteen. She had been through deeper valleys than most people ever know. Looking at Emily would bring anyone to tears, even my father.

The judge who presided over Emily's placement was a close friend of my parents. As an attorney, my father had appeared before this judge many times pursuing adoption for a number of children. The judge told Emily in no uncertain terms that this was her final opportunity before permanently being sent to juvenile detention. I remember him telling Emily, "I am giving you the greatest break of your life. I know this family, and I know they will love you. Don't waste this incredible opportunity." The judge reminded us that foster care is a messy, challenging, rewarding experience that will test our resolve to love but will also bring untold blessing as we give ourselves away. With that word of encouragement, we left the courtroom with Emily as a part of our family.

Emily was a known runner who would look for any opportunity to escape her foster family and run back to her drug-addicted fellow gang members. We understood that one of our initial tasks was to never let Emily out of our sight. We literally watched her 24/7. It was not until we were convinced she was asleep that we would go to bed. It was an exhausting exercise in family teamwork.

My parents went to extreme lengths to assure Emily that she was a part of the family. Soon after she arrived, our family took a picture for our church directory. Naturally, Emily was in the picture as a part of the family. My father framed the picture and hung it in his office. She was a part of our annual family vacation. After the first month, I found myself referring to Emily as my little sister. I was genuinely protective of Emily. I genuinely had affection for a girl who had been through more heartache than my teenage mind could comprehend.

After four months, we were convinced that Emily might actually want to stay around, and we were thrilled. My parents had begun to discuss what it would mean to adopt Emily. One day, while my parents were both at work, my brother Kenny and I miscommunicated, and we showered at the same time. When we both came out of our five-minute showers, Emily was gone.

The next days were some of the most painful of my life. Everyone was frantically searching for Emily. Knowing her background, we feared for not only her safety but also her life. Our family and the Wichita police searched all the regular locations Emily was known to frequent. After three days of searching, I found Emily in a park, huffing gasoline with her friends. When she saw me, she broke into a run. After a short chase (she was high and wasn't moving too quickly), I wrapped my arms around her and told her we were going home. However, when the police learned that Emily had been found, they picked her up and took her straight to a juvenile detention center.

Later that night, my father and I visited Emily. As Emily entered the room and sat at a table across from my father, I heard a sound I had never heard before. My father began to weep uncontrollably. The heart of a man who had been raised in poverty in Oklahoma, served in the Navy, and put himself through law school had been ripped in two by a child. Before then, I had considered my father an unemotional man. Not after that night.

The judge, for some unknown reason, returned Emily to our home. And not long after, Emily ran again. This time, the judge sentenced Emily to juvenile detention until she aged out of the system.

Showing compassion and mercy to Emily was a significant

paradigm shift for my family. Our brief time with her, as painful as it was, intensified our desire to step into the chaotic world of foster care. Not long after Emily departed, Natalie moved in, beginning another chapter of a story. The Lord used the tragic lives of Emily and Natalie to place a deep longing within my heart to care for abandoned children. My wife, Sally, and I are immensely blessed with three biological children. We have also been immeasurably blessed to welcome two adopted children into our family. As with Renaut's family, we did so because we believe that adoption is a beautiful reflection of the gospel call.

The Call of Mercy

Every pastor has their favorite benediction. *Benediction* is a Latin word that simply means "speak well," "good word," or "good wishes." Though benedictions are often from Scripture, they do not have to be, as is the case with my favorite benediction. It speaks directly to the issue of justice:

> Now go into the world in peace. Have courage; hold on to those things that are true, right, and good. Honor all people, because all people have been created in the image of God. Strengthen the fainthearted, support the weak, help the suffering, share the gospel. Love and serve the Lord in the power of the Holy Spirit. And may the grace, mercy, and peace of our Lord Jesus Christ be with you, both today and forevermore. Shalom. Amen.

At the heart of the benediction is a prayer for justice: "honor all people, because all people have been created in the image of

God. Strengthen the fainthearted, support the weak, and help the suffering." We do not love others just so they will become followers of Jesus (though we pray this is an outcome). We do not love others so that they will begin attending our church (though we would welcome them with open arms). We do not love others so that they will become peace-loving, law-abiding, productive citizens in our community (though this is a wonderful result). We fundamentally love people because they have been miraculously and wonderfully created in God's perfect image. While sin would soon corrupt that image, the original state of mankind was not one of sin.

The call to love kindness is the call to demonstrate mercy to all. I generally despise stories where I emerge as a good guy, because I am as broken as the next person. I am a broken, sinful man who desperately needs God's kindness and mercy as much as anyone. With that understood, the following story is an incredible reminder of how simple acts of kindness can change the world.

Many people have horror stories about airlines overbooking flights. I personally witnessed a surreal one. I was aboard an American Airlines flight, returning from a conference in Trinidad and Tobago. It was midafternoon in Raleigh-Durham as I settled into the final leg of my flight home, when an airline representative approached the man next to me. She began a low-level conversation with him. Suddenly, the man raised his voice and said, "But you can't kick me off this flight! My daughter is getting married tonight and I will miss the wedding!"

Now, if you are going to make up a story, I must admit, that was an exceptional one. I asked the man if his daughter was really about to married or if that was just one of the most creative on-the-spot lies I had ever heard. It didn't take long for him to convince me she was. His only daughter was getting married in three hours, and this flight would allow him to barely arrive in time to walk his only daughter down the aisle. I informed the airline representative that I would gladly take his place and voluntarily deplane so he could make his daughter's wedding. It was nothing heroic, just a simple act of kindness.

The man was stunned. "Why would you do that?" he asked. I explained that no father should have to miss his daughter's wedding. As I prepared to deplane, he asked for my card. I happened to have one in my wallet. I handed him my card, called my wife, and told her I would be a couple of hours late. I was happy to help a fellow father. It was a minor inconvenience. It was an opportunity to serve a person in need, and I did what most people would have done. Honestly, I soon forgot about the encounter. (And as it turns out, my kindness was immediately rewarded when I was bumped up to first class on the next flight.)

One month later, a man approached me after I had preached my morning message in the local church I pastored. I recognized the man but couldn't place where I had met him. Tears began to flow as the man began to share his story. He told me about his daughter's wedding and how a stranger had given up a seat on a plane, allowing him to attend one of the most important family events of his life. He thanked me and said, "I am not a regular in church. In fact, I haven't been to church in years. I came here today because of what you did for me."

A simple act of kindness.

The Myth of Safety

While encouraging the local church to engage in ministries of mercy and justice, I am commonly asked about safety. (Frankly, many of the questions are born out of systemic racism.) What if my family engages in a foster care or homeless ministry and one of my children is harmed? What if we are serving in a low-income part of town and I am robbed? How can we practice the ministry of hospitality when we don't know if a refugee could be a terrorist? What if I unknowingly adopt a special needs child? What if we take in a foster child who has an attachment disorder?

Make no mistake, safety is a myth. You don't know what the remainder of this day holds. It is right to take a risk for the cause of Christ. The Christian life is a call to risk. I love one of the mantras of Renaut's church, shared earlier: "We would rather serve at the cost of surviving than survive at the cost of serving."

The gospel reminds us that Jesus Christ left the safety of His position next to the heavenly Father. He came as an immigrant to a lost and dying world. He came to provide an eternal home to those who would follow after Him. May the Lord lead you as you go to the darkest places in our communities and engage that darkness with the message of redemption and the penetrating light of Jesus Christ. We were once refugees, and Jesus gave us a home. We were once orphans, and the Lord adopted us into His family. We were once walking in the darkness of ignorance, and the Lord shined the truth of the gospel into our hearts. Jesus is full of justice, mercy, and kindness. Because of that, we are forever changed.

SELF-ASSESSMENT

On a scale of 1 to 5, how developed are you in the competency of mercy and justice?

1	2	3	4	5
"I admit I am clueless in this competency."	"I know enough to know what I don't know."	"I can get by."	"I have a healthy skill set in this competency."	"I'm killing it in this area."

CHAPTER 24

GENEROSITY

The call came from Dean, a North Carolina pastor. Dean explained that his elders had asked him to preach a series of messages on money. The church was running a financial deficit, and the elders believed that an emergency four-week stewardship series was necessary to pull the church out of the red.

Dean dreaded talking about money from the pulpit. First, he feared that a stewardship series would only magnify the congregation's guilt and shame, triggering a mass departure and ultimately threatening the very life of the church. Second, Dean's own finances were in disarray. He felt woefully inadequate to preach about an area where he mightily struggled.

Because Dean felt as if he had no choice but to preach the series, our conversation centered around how to make the best of the opportunity before him. Dean was clear on the introduction to the series. He would begin by apologizing to any guests who happened to be present. Dean would acknowledge that money is a minefield and that the church regularly stayed away from hazardous polarizing topics. He would explain that he hoped (and prayed) they would return at a later date to hear him preach on something other than money.

I challenged Dean to begin with exactly the opposite approach. I encouraged him to begin his message by welcoming any guests with the following invitation: "If you are a guest this morning looking for a church home and you are here to 'check us out,' you absolutely could not have picked a better service to attend! I invite you to return for all four messages in this series, because what we as a congregation believe about money will reveal more about this church than nearly any other message."

When the topic is money, our hearts are never neutral. Simply speaking the word "money" reminds a portion of the population of unpaid bills, credit card balances, and nonexistent retirement accounts. For some, the thought of money creates defensiveness. For others, money creates pride and a feeling of safety. For most, money is tied to identity, self-worth, and security. The good news is that biblical generosity frees us to live as redeemed sons and daughters of the King, possessed by nothing because as stewards (and not owners) of God's good gifts, we ultimately possess nothing. The Lord desires to free people from the twisted motives espoused by our culture and allow them to enjoy the life-changing freedom of releasing our vice grip on money.

Liberating Generosity

Remember the story of the widow's mite in the Gospels? Jesus sees the rich putting their offerings into the temple treasury, followed by the poor widow who puts in all she has. Jesus tells His disciples, "I tell you, this poor widow has put more into the treasury than all the others. They all gave out of their wealth; but she, out of her poverty, put in everything . . ." (Mark 12:43b–44 NIV). In one sense, Jesus appears to be wrong: the rich actually gave more money. But in the most important sense, Jesus is right: the woman's gift cost more.

One thing people often wonder about this story, though, is doesn't it border on irresponsible for the woman to give all she had to live on? If I gave away everything, I would become a burden on others!

The story is not about financial planning; it's about radical generosity and profoundly humble faith. Many fail to give not because of lack of desire, but because of crushing fear. We convince ourselves that our financial future is more secure by hoarding God's resources now. The woman trusted God with all she possessed. By giving everything, she experienced a freedom that few people will ever know. She considered worshiping God through an act of generosity in the present to be of greater importance than clinging to financial security in the future.

I was never taught this in my early years of ministry. I failed to acknowledge and applaud the gift of faith when I knew that the ones giving were making an incredible sacrifice to give. I failed to see that the most radical financial gifts sometimes come in the form of monetarily small packages. I have come to understand that generosity is a reflection of one's heart.

In 1992, Sally and I moved to Kansas City to plant a church. Moving from South Carolina to Kansas, where we were both born and raised, was a dream come true. One challenging part of planting a church was raising a staggering amount of money that would allow us to move, gather a core group, and launch the church. I will never forget the day that the largest financial gift was given.

> Sacrifices are more valuable than contributions.

Now, don't get me wrong, some families gave incredible sacrificial gifts. Sally and I were deeply humbled by friends who gave gifts larger than our annual income. And yet, the largest gift came from an unlikely source: a twelve-year-old boy.

Roger approached us in August to tell us that he was excited about our call to plant a church in Kansas City. He went on to tell us that he was just learning to mow lawns, and that over the summer he had earned a grand total of $62.50. He handed me a baggie full of small bills and coins. He said, "This is everything I earned this summer. It isn't much, but I want to give it all." *He gave it all.* I still get tears in my eyes when I recount that story. It is no surprise that the Lord is now using Roger in a high-responsibility position directing emergency medical relief efforts around the world. While Roger's gift wasn't the largest monetary gift we received, when evaluated by the standard of Jesus, Roger gave more than anyone.

Teaching about generosity doesn't apply to only the financially wealthy. Sacrifices are more valuable than contributions. According to Jesus, the young couple living from paycheck to paycheck can practice generosity as much as the seasoned couple making a seven-figure income. When Jesus applauds the generosity of the widow, He makes clear that motive of the heart reflects the value of the gift. It is possible to give the Lord our wealth but withhold our heart. Paul affirms this when he says, "If I give all that I have . . . but have not love, I gain nothing" (1 Cor. 13:3). In other words, *means + motive = true level of generosity.*

Generosity and the Church

While it may feel like America is the radically generous, in baseball terms, when everyone on the team is hitting a dismal .190 and you hit .210, comparatively it looks like you're smacking the cover off the ball. I have been privileged to see radical commitment on many occasions, and it is seldom in America. I have seen a friend walk away from a comfortable life in America to pastor in one of the poorer communities of Haiti. As I detailed in the chapter on missions, I have seen an underground seminary in China where students live in a six-room house to prepare for a life of service to the Lord, making a three-year commitment to never leave the house.

I have long appreciated the words of Andy Stanley, who said that preaching on money is an opportunity to tell your congregation what you want *for* them rather than what you want *from* them. Teaching about money is critical to the spiritual maturity of any believer. Addressing issues around money should be a regular part of any church's preaching, because it was a regular part of Jesus' teaching. Sixteen of Jesus' thirty-eight parables are focused on money and possessions. In the four gospels, one out of ten verses (288 in all) address the subject of money. While the Bible gives us five hundred verses on prayer, it gives us more than two thousand on money and possessions.

Many churches avoid asking their members to give sacrificially, fearing that a call to a biblical standard of generosity will drive people away. What many pastors fail to understand is that a high bar of commitment is immensely attractive, particularly to millennials who are drawn to significance over substance. Furthermore, if the church's attitude toward money, spending, and giving is no different than the general population, what do we have to offer the world? A materialistic world will never be won to Christ by a materialistic church.

Far too many in the local church believe that tithing is exclusively a part of the Old Testament law and that in fulfilling the law (Matt. 5:19–21), Jesus displaced the need to give. But tithing did not originate as part of the Old Testament law. Tithing began 430 years before the law was given, when Abraham offered tithes of everything he owned. In fact, tithing goes as far back as Cain and Abel, when Abel, the first tither, offered his firstfruits to the Lord. Tithing was practiced before the law, under the law, and after the law's fulfillment. Jesus never lowered the standard of the tithe. In fact, He raised it to new, unheard-of levels of radical generosity (Luke 3:11).

As a leader, help the church in their financial planning by asking the following three questions:

1. Five minutes after you die, what will you wish you had given?

2. What is your financial finish line—what do you need to care for your family? This is a paradigm-shifting question, as the issue changes from, "How much do I need to give?" to a radical, "How much do I need to keep?"

3. What keeps you from making a commitment to give back to God everything that comes in above your financial finish line?

For many, the thought of a financial finish line is new. A story is told about John Wesley, who, in 1728 at the age of twenty-five, received his first ministry salary of twenty pounds. Wesley lived on eighteen pounds, giving two pounds to the local church. Years later, when Wesley became a well-known evangelist, his income increased to two hundred pounds a year. Wesley lived on eighteen pounds, giving 182 pounds to the local church. Wesley had a financial finish line.

While we are commanded to care for our family (1 Tim. 5:8), we need to understand that an increase in income is an opportunity, not to correspondingly raise our standard of living, but to grow in generosity. The primary purpose of money in Scripture is generosity (2 Cor. 8:1–15). Randy Alcorn instructs believers not to renounce treasure, but to relocate it when he says "you can't take it with you—but you *can* send it on ahead."[40] Don't abandon the idea of storing up treasures for yourself—just put it where it'll last.

The Lottery: What Might Have Been

Many have wrestled with one of the deepest questions in life: What would you do with the money if you won the lottery? While most convince themselves that no amount of money would change the core of who they are, stories of lives destroyed by the sudden influx of money abound.

One fall night in 1985, my wife, Sally, and I were enjoying our regular midweek date night, sitting in a laundromat in a northern suburb of Boston. I was pursuing a master's degree at Gordon-Conwell Theological Seminary, and Wednesday night was laundry night. As we washed our clothes, I couldn't help but notice a long line of people standing outside the liquor store next door. Curious, and incredibly naïve, I ventured outside to find out the cause of the excitement. I approached a gentleman and asked what would cause so many people to stand in line on a chilly fall New England night. He looked at me with shaming eyes and said, "Seriously, you don't know? The Megabucks lottery is 21 million dollars!" (Nowadays, jackpots are even bigger. But in 1985, the Massachusetts lottery was $21,714,520—the largest in US history.)

I returned to the laundromat and informed Sally that all those foolish people were in line to play the lottery. My diatribe went something like this: "What a terrible waste of money! What shallow fool would waste his money gambling on something as stupid as the lottery? But, if we were to play, what six numbers would you choose?" Sally immediately protested, "We are not playing the lottery!" Ignoring her protest, I informed her that I would choose her birthday, my birthday, and our wedding anniversary, in numerical order—1, 2, 6, 10, 18, 28. She again let me know that we would not be playing the lottery.

At the end of our date, we had four quarters remaining. Ignoring my wife's better judgment, I went next door, handed the clerk four quarters, and purchased my first lottery ticket. I stuck it in my wallet and we headed home.

That night, a local Boston station interrupted regular programming for a live broadcast of the lottery drawing. The record-breaking jackpot made this a special occasion. Sally was asleep when the thirty-six balls began bouncing (remember, this is 1985). I casually pulled out my lottery ticket, already feeling foolish for wasting money on such an ill-advised game. The first ball to roll down the chute was 6. The second was 2. "That's funny" I thought to myself, "I'm two for two." The third ball was 28. Three for three. The next ball was 10. I began shaking Sally, "Wake up, sweetheart! We have matched all four balls." The next ball that rolled down the ramp was 1. Five for five! At this point I was screaming! "Sally, wake up!! If the next ball is 18, we're millionaires!" I knelt in front of the television, drool running down my chin, my heart rate rapidly climbing. The last ball began rolling and I screamed, "We won! We won!" And then I took a closer look. As the ball came to a stop, I could see that the final number was not 18. It was 19. We had matched the first five numbers and missed the final number by one. In other words, it would be impossible to come any closer and not win.

I don't know what someone wins today for matching five out of six numbers, but in 1985, the prize was $400. We used $200 to buy our first VCR. We sent the remaining $200 to missionaries because we felt so guilty!

It's a funny story—if it would have ended there. Because of my greed and my appetite for more, for the next several weeks, all I could think about was 21 million dollars. I sat in seminary classes, staring at the professor and thinking, "21 million dollars . . ." I sat at stoplights, as if in a trance, thinking about 21 million dollars. A couple of weeks after our near miss, exasperated, I asked Sally, "Whose senseless idea was it to get married on Saturday (June 18)? If we had married on Sunday (June 19), we'd be rich!"

I remember the day I couldn't take it anymore. In Mark 8:36 Jesus says, "For what does it profit a man to gain the whole world and forfeit his soul?" We had not won the jackpot. We didn't have millions, and yet those millions were controlling my life. I fell to my knees and cried out to God, "Who shall rescue me from this body of death? Thanks be to God who gives me the victory through Jesus Christ my Lord."

The lesson of 1985 continues to this day. P. T. Barnum was right, "Money . . . is a very excellent servant but a terrible master."[41] When we allow money to control our life, we miss out on the incredible liberating freedom that comes when we realize it all belongs to the Lord (Ps. 24:1).

The key to generosity in your life and in your church's life is a deeper understanding of the Lord's generosity. We give as a response to God's tender mercies and generous provisions. Throughout the Scriptures, the motivation for generosity is always tied to Christ's work upon the cross. The Scriptures paint a picture of an elaborately generous God. God generously gives us wisdom

(James 1:5); God grants us life abundantly (John 10:10); He fills our cup until it overflows (Ps. 23:5); He generously gives good gifts to His children (Matt. 7:11); God's mercy is abundant (Ps. 51:1). Ephesians 1:3–8 reminds us that God the Father has blessed us with every spiritual blessing and that we have redemption through the riches of His grace, which He lavished upon us. This is not a picture of a scarcity-mentality God. This is a picture of plentiful generosity from an abundantly kind heavenly Father.

Scholars tell us that when Mary generously anointed Jesus' feet with oil (John 12:3), the pure nard would have been so potent, so lavishly poured upon Jesus that the smell would have stayed with Him all through the trial and the crucifixion. When Joseph took Jesus' body down from the cross, His body would have smelled sweet. That sweetness should remind us of the generous and lavish nature of Jesus, our eternal treasure, who gave it all for His followers.

Teach the people of God to be generous. Call them to a high standard. Regularly teach and preach the blessing of generosity.

SELF-ASSESSMENT

On a scale of 1 to 5, how developed are you in the competency of generosity?

1	2	3	4	5
"I admit I am clueless in this competency."	"I know enough to know what I don't know."	"I can get by."	"I have a healthy skill set in this competency."	"I'm killing it in this area."

PART VI DISCUSSION QUESTIONS

1. On a scale of one to five (five being mastery), how developed are you in the core competency of growing the body of believers?

2. Of the sub-competencies (theology of missions, reproducing and revitalizing the local church, mercy and justice, generosity), which is your strongest? Which is your weakest?

3. What is one way you can lean into your strongest sub-competencies?

4. What is a practice you can implement this week to grow in your weakest sub-competencies?

5. Who could you partner with to cover your weaknesses and minister more effectively together?

ACKNOWLEDGMENTS

A huge thank-you to Drew Dyck and the team at Moody Publishers for believing in pastors and caring about this project. You have a long history of serving pastors and the local church in the USA and around the world. Thank you for swimming in the deep end of the pool.

Thank you to our editing team, particularly Amanda Quain and Matthew Boffey.

Thanks to Andrew Wolgemuth for being a great friend and agent. We could not have walked this road without your wisdom and guidance.

Thanks to Jim Fenlason for your passion to see this book in the hands of pastors. This book would not have happened apart from your dedication and commitment.

Above all, we are particularly grateful to the Lord Jesus, our Redeemer, Savior, and King. Your unending commitment to love pastors and ministry leaders causes us to stand in wonder before Your throne of grace. We pray this book glorifies Your Name, advances Your kingdom agenda, and blesses the church and those whom You have called to lead. *Soli Deo Gloria.*

From Renaut:

In many ways, I have only discovered what I've written in this book because of the life I've shared with my amazing wife, Brooke, and our eight children, Birhanu, Hadley, Fitsimti, Mehari, Cullen, Hope, Rahel, and Cole. Loving you is the greatest work I will ever have the privilege of doing. Thank you for sharing life with me.

Thank you to my parents, Marius and Marian van der Riet. Growing up with Lize and Karen in that little church in Kimberley, South Africa, and watching you live with integrity gave me the foundational knowledge on which my life and ministry are built.

In the same vein, it has been an extraordinary privilege to get to live on mission alongside the men and women who serve Mosaic Church passionately every day. I would have nothing to share in these pages if not for you and the other churches, leaders, mentors, and pastors from around the world with whom I have been able to work and from whom I have learned so much.

Thank you, too, to Jennifer Wylie Fauser and Amanda Quain. Your writing abilities have brought to life most of what I've ever tried to put on paper, and my portion of this book would not have ended up in print without you.

Thanks also to my awesome graphic artist, Kevin Richardson, who nailed the front cover design.

Jimmy, I still don't get why on earth you would want the sharing of this incredible material to be left in my hands when you are the expert, but I'm incredibly honored that you asked me to partner with you in these pages. Your passion for pastors and ministry leaders inspires me. Thank you. It has been an incredible journey.

From Jimmy:

First and foremost, thank you to my incredible wife Sally for her love, encouragement, and faithful support through four decades of ministry together. I could not have asked for a better best friend, spouse, and partner in life and ministry. In the words of Anne Shirley, you are my *really kindred spirit to whom I can confide my inmost soul.* Our kids hit a home run when they got you as their mom! I love you.

Thank you to my family for their consistent love, patience, and support. Paige and Allie, thanks for allowing your Dad to sneak away to write a book. And thanks for occasionally allowing me to win a game of Rummikub.

A huge thank-you to my coauthor Renaut. Writing with a dear friend who loves pastors as you do is an incredible privilege. I have such respect for you as a pastor and a leader, but I am awe-struck as I watch you love and care for Brooke and your eight children. Your backstage exceeds your frontstage. That is the highest compliment I can give a gifted leader like yourself.

Thank you to the PastorServe team for the joy you bring me each day as I am allowed to serve alongside you. Each of you have significantly contributed to the contents of this book. I am especially grateful to Clark Tanner, Bryant Lee, Brian Brookins, Kesnel Joseph, Jeanne Martin, Rick Pierce and Lainie MacDonald. In particular, thank-you to my amazing coworker Jay Fowler for your enormous help with the conflict material. Thank you to Arthur Jackson for your powerful insights and assistance with the mercy and justice chapter. Thank you to the PastorServe board for encouraging me in the writing of this book, particularly Cathryn Moyes and Scott Hickox.

A big thank-you to my dear friends and partners at Nehemiah 3.

This journey has largely been made possible because of your generosity.

Much of my writing flows out of the joy and care that comes from a close circle of friends. Thanks to Brent Becker, Bruce McGregor, Rick McNabb, Andy Moyes, Justin Moxley, Eddie Copeland, Lance Witt, Mindy Caliguire, Stephan Tchividjian, Brad Wells, John Brooks, Jeremiah Enna, and Dayton Moore. Your friendship blesses me beyond what you will ever know.

Finally, a heartfelt thank you to Gary Ascanio, my most faithful prayer partner who daily prays that the Lord will use me beyond what I could ask or imagine.

NOTES

1. Richard J. Krejcir, "Statistics on Pastors," Into Thy Word, 2007, http://www.intothyword.org/apps/articles/?articleid=36562.

2. Melissa Steffan, "Three Megachurch Pastors Resign over Adultery in Orlando," *Christianity Today*, May 16, 2013, https://www.christianitytoday.com/news/2013/may/three-megachurch-pastors-resign-over-adultery-in-orlando.html.

3. William Carey, Joshua Marshman, William Ward, "The Bond of the Missionary Brotherhood of Serampore, in George Smith, *The Life of William Carey* (London: John Murray, 1885), 450.

4. Richard Foster, *Celebration of Discipline: The Path to Spiritual Growth* (New York: HarperCollins, 1998), 33.

5. Ibid., 7.

6. Ibid., 55.

7. Dave Huber, "Avodah Word Study," EFCA Today, https://www.efcatoday.org/story/avodah-word-study.

8. Nicola Magnavita and Serio Garbarino, "Sleep, Health and Wellness at Work: A Scoping Review," *International Journal of Environmental Research and Public Health* 14, no. 11 (2017): 1347, https://www.ncbi.nlm.nih.gov/pmc/articles/PMC5707986/.

9. "Blue Light Has a Dark Side," *Harvard Health Letter*, Harvard Health Publishing, July 2, 2020, https://www.health.harvard.edu/staying-healthy/blue-light-has-a-dark-side.

10. James Bryan Smith, *The Good and Beautiful God: Falling in Love with the God Jesus Knows* (Downers Grove, IL: IVP Books, 2009), 142.

11. "The KJV Old Testament Hebrew Lexicon," s.v. "Shama`," Bible Study Tools, https://www.biblestudytools.com/lexicons/hebrew/kjv/shama.html.

12. John Calvin, quoted in Ed Stetzer, "Mission, Self, and God's Glory (Part 1)," *Christianity Today*, August 4, 2014, https://www.christianitytoday.com/edstetzer/2014/august/mission-self-and-gods-glory-part-1.html.

13. N. T. Wright, *Surprised by Hope: Rethinking Heaven, the Resurrection, and the Mission of the Church* (New York: HarperOne, 2008), 182.

14. I am indebted to the Kansas Leadership Center in Wichita, Kansas, led by Ed O'Malley, for their research into dynamic leadership. While I have learned countless leadership truths at the feet of KLC mentors, the concept of technical work vs. adaptive work is the most important.

15. Jimmy Dodd and Larry Magnuson, *Pastors Are People Too* (Colorado Springs, CO: David C. Cook, 2016), 36.

16. Marc Levy, *If Only It Were True* (New York: Pocket Books, 2000), 194–95.

17. Bob Burns, Tasha D. Chapman, and Donald C. Guthrie, *Resilient Ministry* (Downers Grove, IL: IVP Books, 2013), 26.

18. I am grateful for the opportunity to write with Renaut, whom I consider to be a uniquely gifted leader. Renaut's church does leadership development incredibly well. Mosaic's executive pastor, Phil Taylor, has compiled a highly effective church leadership training process. A portion of the following has been extracted from his materials.

19. In the context of the local church, an elder team is first and foremost a group of shepherds. Everything else is secondary and optional. (See chapter 19 on the role of shepherding.) Each elder uniquely brings different gifts to build up the body of believers. In addition to meeting the biblical requirements (1 Tim. 3:1–7), they should possess a passion for justice, the nations, unreached people groups, and the lost. Elders should weep over the lost as the Lord Jesus wept over Jerusalem. The office of elder demands that one is closely walking with the Holy Spirit.

20. Burns, Chapman, Guthrie, *Resilient Ministry*, 250.

21. Winston Churchill, "We Shall Fight on the Beaches," International Churchill Society, June 4, 1940, https://winstonchurchill.org/resources/speeches/1940-the-finest-hour/we-shall-fight-on-the-beaches/.

22. It is not my intention in this brief discussion of community to touch on the distinction between small communities of believers and the house church. I am well aware of the house church movement in the United States and around the world. I applaud the growth of the house church, particularly in areas of the world where a larger gathering of believers is difficult or even problematic.

23. Rick Warren, *The Purpose Driven Life: What on Earth Am I Here For?* (Grand Rapids: Zondervan, 2002), 163.

24. Brandon Webb, "Naval Special Warfare Command," SOFREP, December 28, 2011, https://sofrep.com/specialoperations/nswc/.

25. "SEAL Ethos," Naval Special Warfare, https://www.nsw.navy.mil/NSW/SEAL-Ethos/.

26. George Barna, *Growing True Disciples: New Strategies for Producing Genuine Followers of Christ* (Colorado Springs, CO: WaterBrook, 2001); quoted in Gary, "Discipleship Materials Easy to Use," *Your Journey Blog with Gary Rohrmayer,* https://garyrohrmayer.typepad.com/yourjourneyblog/discipleship-materials-easy-to-use.html.

27. Eugene H. Peterson, *A Long Obedience in the Same Direction: Discipleship in an Instant Society* (Downers Grove, IL: IVP Books, 2000), 127.

28. Deitrich Bonhoeffer, *The Cost of Discipleship* (1937; repr., New York: Touchstone, 1995), 89.

29. Ibid., 36.

30. For an excellent understanding of confession and forgiveness, see Ken Sande, *The Peacemaker: A Biblical Guide to Resolving Personal Conflict* (Grand Rapids: Baker Books, 2004).

31. Lindy Lowry, "215 Million Believers Face Persecution for Their Faith in Christ," Open Doors USA, January 10, 2018, https://www.opendoorsusa.org/christian-persecution/stories/215-million-believers-persecution-for-their-faith-in-christ/.

32. "The Truth about the 1969 Woodstock Music Festival," History by Day, https://www.historybyday.com/pop-culture/the-truth-about-the-1969-woodstock-music-festival/49.html.

33. Os Guinness, *Dining with the Devil: The Megachurch Movement Flirts with Modernity* (Grand Rapids: Hourglass Book, 1993), 90.

34. Ibid.

35. Stephen A. Macchia, *Becoming a Healthy Church: Ten Traits of a Vital Ministry* (Grand Rapids: Baker Books, 1999), 228.

36. From Redeemer Presbyterian Church's "Vision and Values" page, accessed October 4, 2020, www.redeemer.com/learn/about_us/vision_and_values/.

37. "Research Shows Black Drivers More Likely to Be Stopped by Police," NYU, May 5, 2020, https://www.nyu.edu/about/news-publications/news/2020/may/black-drivers-more-likely-to-be-stopped-by-police.html.

38. Kimberly Kahn et al., "Racial Bias in Drivers' Yielding Behavior at Crosswalks: Understanding the Effect," NITC-RR-869, Portland, OR: Transportation Research and Education Center (TREC), October 2017, https://doi.org/10.15760/trec.185.

39. Jon C. Rogowski and Cathy J. Cohen, "Black Millennials in America," Black Youth Project, https://blackyouthproject.com/wp-content/uploads/2015/11/BYP-millenials-report-10-27-15-FINAL.pdf.

40. Randy Alcorn, *The Treasure Principle: Unlocking the Secret of Joyful Giving,* revised and updated (Colorado Springs, CO: Multnomah, 2017), 100.

41. P. T. Barnum, *The Art of Money Getting or, Golden Rules for Making Money* (1880; repr., Compass Circle, 2020), 27.

ABOUT THE AUTHORS

Renaut van der Riet

Renaut van der Riet loves to go zip-lining with his eight kids through the backyard adventure course they built together. He loves snorkeling and tasting new foods with Brooke, his wife of twenty five years, and he loves their family's Saturday-morning waffle breakfast buffets.

He walks quickly. He talks with his hands and his arms. He drinks a lot of coffee. And if you find yourself at his home, you're likely to see him carrying heavy bags of food for the chickens or tilling soil, because Brooke loves gardening.

Renaut is also a pastor, church planter, entrepreneur, and community leader. In 2002, Renaut and Brooke founded Mosaic Church in Winter Garden, Florida. With a congregation now in the thousands, Mosaic has become a nationwide pacemaker for fostering and adoption and a sought-after model of how ministries can respond to children with special needs.

In 2009, he started Love Made Visible, a nonprofit organization that equips families, individuals, churches, and agencies to care for orphans and vulnerable children across the United States and around the world. The following year, he and Brooke founded Axum Coffee Company, a growing chain of coffee shops and restaurants whose goal is to fund church planting and justice-and-mercy initiatives. It is named after the city in Ethiopia from which they adopted four of their children.

Most recently, Renaut is developing The ReStory, a website aimed at providing gospel clarity to followers of Christ by inviting them to tumble headfirst into the wonder of the freedom for which Christ has set them free.

Jimmy Dodd

Jimmy Dodd (BA, Wheaton College; MDiv, Gordon-Conwell Seminary) is the founder and CEO of PastorServe. Serving across denominational lines, PastorServe exists to strengthen the church by serving pastors. Jimmy pastored in Wheaton, IL; Lexington, MA; and Greenville, SC, before planting a church in Kansas City in 1992. Jimmy served for ten years on the teaching team at Woodmen Valley Chapel in Colorado Springs.

Jimmy is the author of *Survive or Thrive: 6 Relationships Every Pastor Needs, Pastors Are People Too* (with Larry Magnuson), and the children's book *The Magnificent Names of Jesus* (with Sally Dodd).

In 2000, Jimmy helped launch Cross International, a ministry devoted to serving the poorest of the poor around the world.

Jimmy and his wife, Sally, have five children and five grandchildren. Two of their daughters were adopted from China. In his free time, Jimmy enjoys reading, talking walks with Sally and their dog, Finn, and cheering on his beloved Jayhawks at Allen Fieldhouse in Lawrence, KS.

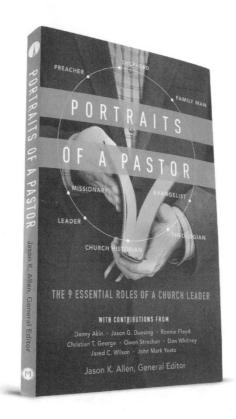

IT'S A QUESTION HUNDREDS OF PASTORS ASK EVERY DAY: WHAT IS THE BEST WAY TO GROW?

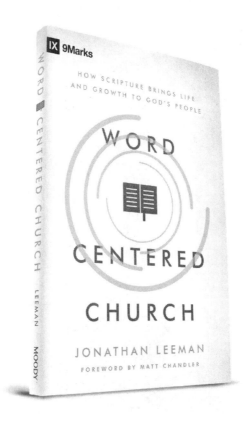

MOODY Publishers®

From the Word to Life®

Theological and practical, *Word-Centered Church* focuses on how the church hears, responds to, discusses, implements, and is transformed by Scripture. It is the ministry-model book that churches need because it advances the model God designed. For anyone who wants to grow or help others grow, *Word-Centered Church* is indispensable.

978-0-8024-1559-2 | also available as an eBook

STUDY THE BIBLE WITH PROFESSORS FROM MOODY BIBLE INSTITUTE

PASTOR, IT'S TIME TO TURN DOWN THE NOISE AND FOCUS ON WHAT MATTERS.